WHAT DO YOU SEEK?

JESUS ANSWERS MODERN MAN

Fr. William F. Maestri

Foreword by
Rev. John Shea

Our Sunday Visitor, Inc.
Huntington, Indiana 46750

Nihil Obstat:
Rev. John H. Miller, C.S.C., S.T.D.
Censor Librorum

Imprimatur:
✝Philip M. Hannan, D.D., J.C.D., S.T.L.
Archbishop of New Orleans
April 24, 1985

The Nihil Obstat and Imprimatur are official declarations that a book or pamphlet is free of doctrinal or moral error. No implication is contained therein that those who have granted the Nihil Obstat or Imprimatur agree with the contents, opinions or statements expressed.

For Sister Mary Henry Simoneaux, R.S.M.

CONTENTS

Part I
Following Jesus

Part II
Loving the Neighbor

FOREWORD

"And no one had the courage to ask him any more questions." (Mark 12:34)

IT IS NOW Jesus' turn, and He has a few questions of His own.

It is the special merit of William Maestri's book that he takes seriously the questions of Jesus. He does not dismiss them as mere rhetorical flourishes, nor rush to the expected, pious answer: "Of course, it does not profit a person to gain. . . . Of course, it is the one who sits at table who is the greatest, not the one who. . ." He listens attentively, allowing the questions of the Master to search and seize him. It is what a disciple does.

The New Testament is rich in its praise of Jesus of Nazareth. He is the Logos, Son of God, New Adam, Son of Man, Messiah, Prophet, and much more. Yet each of these diverse titles should not obscure the simple appreciation of Jesus that many of the Gospels' stories suggest. He is a Master, and He is apprenticing His disciples (and anyone who will stop and listen) into the ways of the Kingdom.

We have often translated the master-disciple relationship of Jesus and His friends into a teacher-student relationship. We have then envisioned Jesus giving stand-up monologues on various topics. Jesus teaches a course, complete with imagined blackboard, on poverty, fasting, prayer, pride, ritual habits, etc. But this approach misses the interpersonal dynamics that permeate every page of the Gospels. Jesus does not teach lessons; He encounters people. He does not want to give pithy sayings for all time; He wants the soul of the person directly in front of Him. When Jesus prays, His eyes drift toward heaven. But when He is the Master, "he looked at them and said. . . ."

One of the principal ways Jesus exercised His guru role was through questioning. And to complicate matters, one of Jesus' most annoying habits was to respond to a question with a question. Take this rapid exchange as an example.

> Another time a man came up to him and said, "Teacher, what good must I do to possess eternal life?" He answered, "Why do you question me about what is good? One alone is good." (Mt 19:16-17)

The sharpness of Jesus' reply bothers many people. This man seems to be a sincere seeker. Why is the Master harrassing him?

Because the Master discerns in his question a hidden spiritual center. The "heart," out of which comes good and evil, is hidden. The questions we ask reveal this hidden source of energy and action. The heart of this man is acquisitive. He want to possess eternal life. He does not want to participate in it or receive it like a child. He wants to own it.

At the end of this interchange, we'll find out that he owns many things; "his possessions were many." He wants one more. The trinket he desires is "eternal life."

Jesus' question tries to surface the assumptive world he is working out of but which he is probably unaware of. The strategy of the Master is to unmask what looks like a sincere religious search. The problem that Jesus discerns is that the man is resting in his own goodness and not in the "One who alone is good." The question Jesus puts to him is meant to bring him to this realization.

That is the peculiar genius of questioning. It wants the one questioned to come to an awareness of what the questioner perceives. It does not want to "tell the listener something." Questions help; they do not dictate. They gradually guide the one questioned deeper and deeper into the reality the questioner knows. The master does not make the disciple dependent on the master's insights. He leads the disciple into the reality they both share. In the case of Jesus, this reality is the Kingdom of God. And when the disciple, attentive and struggling, has come into contact with this reality, Jesus calls him no longer servant but friend, because "I have made known to you all I have heard from my Father" (Jn 15:15).

In casual conversation, questions arrive with little incisiveness and very little interest in the answer. "How are you doing?" "What are you doing?" "How much are you making?" "What's new?" To cultivate standarized answers to these questions and stay on this level is to become a disciple of a shallow culture. There is another option.

We can become "third-party" disciples of Jesus. We can watch Him interact with His contemporaries and, through that interaction, question us. Jesus is the first party. The person or persons in the Gospel narrative are the second party. We are the third party. If the questions of Jesus seek the souls of the people in the Gospel stories, their ambition in regard to us is no less.

Discipleship to Jesus is a journey of high adventure.

Bill Maestri's book is a faithful guide.

John Shea
St. Mary of the Lake Seminary
Mundelein, Illinois

INTRODUCTION

WHAT IS IT about Jesus that we find so fascinating? What is it about Jesus that keeps us thirsting for more and more? Even in the '60s with the so-called "death of God" theologies, Jesus continued to be held in high esteem. Many young people of that turbulent decade were turned off by traditional values and institutions, yet they were "turned on" by Jesus. The expression "Jesus-freak" was anything but a put-down. Today's young people continue to find Jesus appealing although they persist in avoiding much of institutional religion. George Gallup's research indicates that today's youth are among the most "spiritual" on record. The young are seeking a living relationship with God; they like to pray, want discipline and moral guidance, and profess strong positive feelings and images toward Jesus. The young usually associate Jesus with such positive terms as "friend," "lover," and "one who cares" about them.

Naturally, this fascination with Jesus is not limited to the young. The attraction of Jesus cuts across the barriers of race, class, education, and age. The appeal of Jesus even extends beyond the boundaries of the various Christian communities into the so-called "other religions" of the East. New and exciting possibilities for dialogue and understanding are taking place, based on the person and

1

teaching of Jesus. The various Christian denominations are reaching out to one another on the basis of their ultimate common bond — Jesus as Lord.

We must ask again: What is it about Jesus that so many find so fascinating? The fascination with Jesus does *not* come from those things we might initially expect: social status, education, economic clout, family connections, world traveling, or human respect. In fact, Jesus was anything but successful if judged by the standards of the world. Our fascination with Jesus must be found elsewhere. The fascination with Jesus comes from the *questions* He asks us. The questions of Jesus touch on the fundamental issues of human existence: the meaning of daily life; the troubling issues of pain, suffering, finitude, and death; the issues of life after death — judgment, heaven, and hell; the struggles to seek the good and do what is right. And Jesus asks the question concerning the Really Real — is God a God of indifference or a God of involvement with His creation; and if God is involved, is His involvement one of malignity or graciousness?

The questions of Jesus are so fascinating and enjoy such widespread appeal because they center on what it means to be a fully alive human being. These questions are the big questions, about fundamental issues, that each person must ask for himself or herself. The professor at Harvard, the adolescent, the priest in the rectory, and the proverbial man in the street ask these questions. We can take flight from asking them, but we never avoid them completely. To refuse these questions about human existence would be like trying to live without breathing. The questions of Jesus — the fundamental questions of human existence — must be answered. To whom shall we go? Who or what will provide meaning and truth for these basic human concerns?

Jesus is not only the One who asks the questions; He is

also *the* One who provides meaning and truth in them. The One who asks is also the One who answers. I must be honest and say that I cannot by rational argument alone convince you of Jesus as the One who provides ultimate meaning and truth. The "gold and silver" of the Gospel cannot be limited to a set of clear and distinct ideas. The conviction that Jesus is Lord and the One who answers the riddle of human existence must risk the venture of faith. This faith is never irrational or a blind leap into the certainties of some ideal future or golden age. Rather, in the best moments of the Catholic tradition, our faith seeks understanding. We constantly stand ready to give an answer for this hope of ours. On the basis of the best available evidence, the loving lives of Christians, we proclaim (not argue or shout) that Jesus is the One who answers the deepest longing of the human heart. Jesus reveals to us what it means to be truly alive. The *total* story of Jesus is one which affirms the graciousness of God and assures us that we can risk loving one another. Jesus assures us that we may dare to call God our Father, love one another as brothers and sisters, and experience a change of heart which opens our eyes to the neighbor in need. Above all, by faith we can proclaim that Jesus answers the deepest questions of the human spirit, as no other philosopher or teacher, because the crucified Jesus is *alive*! The Man of Sorrows, the Man Forsaken by God, now lives. The scandal of the Cross is fully understood in light of the Easter proclamation: "He is risen! Alleluia!"

Please allow me a brief word about biblical spirituality and the notion of invitation. The person, ministry, and questions of Jesus are contained in a library of books we call the Bible. The Bible is not value-free but confronts the reader from a specific perspective or world view. Its books, from Genesis to Revelation, proclaim this truth: God is passionately in love with us and wants to establish a covenant or relationship with us. God is not some distant ruler, some capricious oriental despot; nor is God a watchmaker who creates and forgets about the works of His hands. The Bible tells us God *cares* and is *passionately involved* with His people. God reveals Himself to us because He wants us to enter into covenant with Him. We don't earn this relationship with God. Even less does God have to be "bought off" or appeased by our sacrifices. God freely and lovingly gives Himself to us and demands that we give ourselves to Him and one another. The Bible is the testimony of faith that God makes Himself known and wants a response from us. The acceptable response is not one of money, achievements, wise investments, worldly trophies, or the key to the executive washroom. God wants us! God wants me and you — totally. No substitutes are acceptable.

Hence the spirituality of the Bible is anything but abstract, spiritualistic (as that which stands against the material creation), and escapist. The spirituality of the Bible is earthly, fleshy, human, and concrete. Among the ways in which we come to know and love God is through the realities of everyday life. Unfortunately we so often overlook (or better yet, underlook) the presence of God. In the words of Alan W. Watts:

> God is the most obvious thing in the world. He is absolutely self-evident — the simplest, clearest and closest reality of life and consciousness. We are only unaware of Him because we are too complicated, for our vision is darkened by the complexity of pride. We seek beyond the horizon with our noses lifed high in the air, and fail to see that He lies at our very feet. . . . We are like birds flying in quest of air, or men with lighted candles searching through the darkness for fire. *(Behold the Spirit)*

The nearness of God is beautifully discussed by the priest-scientist Pierre Teilhard de Chardin in *The Divine Milieu*:

> God is as pervasive and perceptible as the atmosphere in
> which we are bathed. He emcompasses us on all sides, like
> the world itself. What prevents you, then, from enfolding
> Him in your arms? Only one thing: your inability *to see
> Him.*

The spirituality of the Bible provides us with the opportunity to experience the unbounded love of God. From the perspective of the Scriptures there is no separation between faith in God and daily life. There is one God, and one world, and one life we have been given. It is in that concrete life, as gift, that we come to know and love God. The questions of Jesus are directed to us in the particular circumstances of our lives. The answers we formulate, and reformulate, flow from meeting Jesus in the 1,001 concerns that make up our day.

The heart of biblical spirituality is the proclamation that God reveals Himself to us. God reveals Himself as Unbounded Lover. The most powerful expression of God as Love is the Cross. But there is more involved. Not only does God reveal Himself as Lover, but He also *invites* us into a love-relationship. The word "invites" is crucial. God respects our freedom. God does not bully or threaten us into covenant. God does not coerce us into following Him.

Love demands the risk of freedom. We have the power to turn away from the One who alone is our peace. We can refuse to respond in love to the God who first loved us. God will not suspend our freedom or hold our souls in angry hands. The tragedy of sin is our refusal to be disciples. Yet we must be clear about this: we may give up on God, others, and ourselves, but God will *never* give up on us. While respecting our freedom, God is a tenacious Lover who *continues* to offer us the possibilities for new life. God is the Divine Artist who lovingly labors to change our hearts of stone to hearts of flesh.

An introduction should alert the reader to coming attractions. The plan of this book is simple. There are three major sections, each containing five questions or chapters.

Each chapter centers upon a particular question of Jesus and its relationship to the spiritual life. The book closes with an epilogue on the meaning of Christian joy. Among the issues under discussion are: the meaning of life, knowing Jesus, loving Jesus, forgiveness, healing, service, authority, love, and meditation on Mary and John the Baptizer. Naturally, the questions and issues selected are by no means exhaustive. These are the questions of Jesus that have fascinated me and have recurred throughout my priestly ministry. More importantly, my reflections on the questions of Jesus are by no means definitive. They are my reflections at this point in my Christian pilgrimage as a human being and a priest. I offer these reflections as a way of sharing faith and inviting others to grow in knowing Jesus. Other questions and other answers are possible. The beauty of God is found in the diversity of gifts united in the one Spirit. If these questions and reflections will help you to know Christ more deeply, then what follows has achieved its goal.

Finally, the writing of a book accomplishes two very important things. Writing helps us to realize how indebted we are to others through their daily living, teaching, and writing. And secondly, writing affords us the opportunity to be grateful by acknowledging a debt. I want to thank Mr. Robert Lockwood of Our Sunday Visitor, Inc., for all his support and help. Thanks also to Father John Shea, who teaches us all so much about the stories of God's love for us. His foreword is much appreciated. A special word of thanks to David Melancon, O.S.B., of St. Joseph Abbey for his "secret" help. To those countless others who have helped me write this book, please know I am grateful. All shortcomings are my own. Finally, I wish to thank Patricia Kives, who so ably typed the manuscript. Your reward will be great in heaven!

With the Introduction and acknowledgments completed, let us turn to the questions of Jesus.

William F. Maestri

Feast of the Ascension, 1985

PART I

Following Jesus

CHAPTER 1

'What are you looking for?' (Jn 1:38)

> The next day John was there again with two of his disciples. As he watched Jesus walk by he said, "Look! There is the Lamb of God!" The two disciples heard what he said, and followed Jesus. When Jesus turned around and noticed them following him, he asked them, "What are you looking for?" They said to him, "Rabbi (which means Teacher), where do you stay?" "Come and see," he answered. So they went to see where he was lodged, and stayed with him that day. (It was about four in the afternoon.) One of the two who had followed him after hearing John was Simon Peter's brother Andrew. The first thing he did was seek out his brother Simon and tell him, "We have found the Messiah!" (This term means the Anointed.) He brought him to Jesus, who looked at him and said, "You are Simon, son of John; your name shall be Cephas (which is rendered Peter)." (John 1:35-42)

THE FIRST of Jesus' questions we shall discuss, and the most fundamental, is contained in the Fourth Gospel. St. John is distinctive in presenting ordinary events, people, and questions that carry extraordinary importance. At first blush the question of Jesus — "What do you seek?" — seems innocent enough. On the most ordinary level, these two disciples of John the Baptizer could be seeking the good life: more fish, bigger boats, favorable weather. Maybe their aspirations were political and nationalistic — to be freed from Roman rule. Of course Jesus means something far greater: What are you looking for? What is it that gives *ultimate* meaning to your life? What moves you out of the bed and propels you through your every day? Jesus is asking these prospective disciples what are the deepest longings of their hearts.

The two disciples are not sure how to respond, but they know that the real answer is somehow associated with the person of Jesus. The disciples have their own question: "Where are you staying?" This is the beginning of discipleship and the first step toward true happiness. The disciple must *want* to be with Jesus. The disciple must *want* to be one with Jesus in word and deed. In order to answer the question — "What do you seek?" — the disciples must dwell with Jesus. If one is sincerely searching for truth, Jesus extends the crucial invitation: "Come and see."

The two disciples are not able to answer the question of Jesus — "What do you seek?" — by themselves. It is only through relationship with Jesus that one can hope to find the answer. The deepest longing of the human heart is God. Apart from God we cannot be truly happy. Apart from God we are forever restless. Jesus is the way to the Father. Why? Jesus and the Father are one. To see Jesus is to see the Father. The ultimate dwelling place of Jesus is with the Father. Jesus "falls from heaven" in order to tell men and women of the Father's love. What do you seek? Only one answer is acceptable — God. Only one way is authentic — following Jesus.

In our brief passage from St. John, two additional elements deserve comment: first, faith always involves a risk, and secondly, faith is a journey into the person of Jesus. The disciples of John ask Jesus, "Where are you staying?" Jesus responds, "Come and see." Jesus does not provide the disciples with a list of guarantees or a beautiful vision of a trouble-free future. Jesus does not speak of sweet certainty but invites the disciples to come and see where He abides. Such an invitation is filled with risk and a good deal of fear that must be overcome. Boats and nets must be left behind. Family relationships cannot stand in the way of the new family of God. Even the beloved John the Baptizer must grow less so Jesus can become all in all. Discipleship has its costs. There is no cheap grace. Discipleship, the risk of dwelling with Jesus, challenges one to leave everything behind. The painful task of recentering one's life is in order.

To accept the invitation and risk of dwelling with Jesus involves the disciple in a *process* of understanding who Jesus is. In other words, the faith-relationship with Jesus takes time. This no doubt proves problematic for our instant-oriented world. We want instant foods, answers, and intimacy. The same holds true for our spirituality. We demand instant conversion, instant knowledge of Jesus, and instant sainthood. The popularity of books and preachers who promise the "quick fix" connection with God are very attractive. However, a genuine relationship with Jesus does not work that way (for that matter, every genuine I-Thou relationship requires time).

John the Baptizer identifies Jesus as "the Lamb of God." This Old-Testament image is one which associates Jesus with the One who saves His people through innocent suffering and death. Jesus is the perfect Paschal Lamb who freely and lovingly is lifted up so that new life can be achieved for the people. The disciples follow Jesus and address him as "Rabbi," which means Teacher or "my great one." It is only after the disciples stay with Jesus that they come to the deepest understanding of who Jesus is: "We have found the Messiah." Jesus is the Christ who will reconcile God and humankind through His death and resurrection. To know Jesus as the Messiah is not a cause for boasting, a privilege, or an escape from the demands of daily life. Andrew knows Jesus as the Messiah and

brings his brother Simon to Jesus. To know and stay with
Jesus is the fulfillment of the heart's deepest longing.
Jesus is the good news, the best news; and one must pro-
claim Jesus to all of one's brothers and sisters.

The question of Jesus — "What do you seek?" — is not
only for the disciples of John and the society of first-century Palestine. With utmost urgency, men and women are
asking the question of meaning today. Fundamental questions of human existence (Why was I born? Why do I do
what I do each day? What is the goal of my life?) are de-
manding an answer. Yet don't answers abound in today's
modern world come of age? Yes, they do; however, more
and more, we find them hollow. The modern age has
hitched its wagon to the stars of science and technology.
We know so much about the physical world. We have ex-
plored the depths of the ocean. We have ventured off
Spaceship Earth and touched other planets and probed distant stars. We have mastered nature and produced an
abundance of material goods to help us live the good life.
The religion of science and the dogma of progress were
supposed to usher us into the Promised Land, heaven on
earth. We moderns have freed ourselves from the illusion
of religion. We proudly proclaim the death of God and the
meaninglessness of tradition. To Jesus' question — What
do we seek? — the answers are clear: a knowledge that
yields power, an abundance of goods and conveniences,
and a life of pleasure that keeps away the boredom. Today
we have turned away from philosophers, saints, poets, and
mystics as role models. It is, as Alasdair MacIntyre indicates is his excellent book *After Virtue*, to the aesthete,
the manager, and the therapist that we look for guidance
in answering the big questions.

Once again, the voices of discontent are being raised.
We are living lives of *not*-so-quiet desperation. The depths
of the human heart cannot be satisfied with knowledge,

goods, and pleasures alone. The human heart is in need of wisdom, the Good, and happiness as well-being or a blessed spirit. The discontent and crises of the modern heart are fundamentally spiritual crises. Pleasure, fame, power, money, and sexual attractiveness are insufficient to fill the human heart. In themselves, these things need not be evil. In themselves, however, they are insufficient. They ignore the spiritual identity and dignity of the human person. What do *you* seek? If you want to serve on the stock market; if you desire an American Express Card; if you want to be a guest on the Tonight Show; or if you want to rule the Playboy empire, then Jesus will disappoint you. None of these is offered. Why? Because Jesus loves us too much and respects our dignity as His own. What Jesus offers us is far greater than the trinkets of Madison Avenue. If your heart desires more and is open to more, then Jesus is the answer.

Once again, the question of Jesus: "What do *you* seek?" J.B. Phillips wrote a popular book, *Your God Is Too Small*, about our images of God being so limited (God as judge, policeman, Santa Claus, etc.). Well, the real smallness lies with the human heart. We are afraid to hope too much, believe too much, and love too much. Yet contained in Jesus' question is the invitation ("Come and see") to find that which alone can make us truly alive and happy — God. Jesus is saying to us, "Come and see. Come and see where I dwell. The Father and I are one. To see me is to see the Father. To love me is to love the Father and we will make our dwelling within you." Jesus is saying that we can hope for God and not be disappointed. Ultimately we will be disappointed if we seek happiness apart from God. Fame is fleeting. "Hail and hosanna!" have a way of becoming "Away with him, crucify him!" Possessions have a way of possessing us. If a thief can steal them, a moth consume them and rust destroy them, how valuable can they be? The powerful are the most dependent. Leaders need followers and masters need slaves. Beauty that is only skin deep withers and succumbs to what Camus called "the cruel mathematics that claims our condition." Apart from God, life is "a tale / Told by an idiot, full of sound and fury, / Signifying nothing." Apart from God we must face death with the cry of rebellion or the whimpering resolution of despair.

Jesus is inviting us to "come and see" a better way. We are invited to a way that leads to God and eternal life. In hearing this, the modern reflex responds: "Isn't Christian hope just dope? The message and invitation of Jesus is just so much opium, which diverts our attention from living in the here and now! The invitation to 'come and see' is an offer to escape the sufferings and injustices of an all too human history and condition." Nothing could be further from the truth. If one is truly seeking God with all of one's heart, and one freely accepts the invitation to dwell with Jesus, then one is fundamentally saying "Yes" to the Cross. This is the realism that our escapist world finds a stumbling block and a scandal. To follow Jesus is not to be excused from living and loving here and now. To be a disciple demands a cost; at times it can be the ultimate cost of one's life. The invitation to "come and see" means that one must journey to Jerusalem. If we try to be a disciples without the Cross, we are asking for the same rebuke Jesus handed Peter! "Get behind me, Satan! You are a hindrance to me; for you are not on the side of God, but of men" (Mt 8:33). The real avoidance and illusion lie with the world and its idols.

Harvard economist John Kenneth Galbraith has termed our period in history "the age of uncertainty." Some would go further and say we are living in the time of "world-darkening." Others proclaim our time as one in which the old gods have died and the new are not yet ap-

pearing. We must be careful about such labels, which are
often libel. Each epoch has its troubles sufficient for the
day. For example, Bernard of Cluny in the twelfth century
wrote:

> The world is very evil
>   The times are waxing late;
> Be sober and keep vigil,
>   The Judge is at the gate.

Yet side by side with such doom and gloom, the twelfth
century experienced a great leap in the quality of life: the
rise of universities, advances in architecture, contact with
the Moslem world, a reappreciation of Greek science, and
the flowering of vernacular literature.

Today the litany of our problems is challenging: nuclear war, terrorism, hunger, poverty, urban violence, the
loss of traditional values and systems of meaning, and the
concerns of energy and ecology. Any one of these by itself
could move us to say "Amen" to the hymn of Bernard. Yet
there is a different voice, a hymn that calls to our hearts.
In the midst of so much shrillness, the quiet invitation of
Jesus is offered to us: "Come and see." Jesus is inviting
us to come and see what life is like when our hearts are
centered in God. The problems of war, violence, meaninglessness, and general inhumanity to one another will not
go away by building bigger bombs, surer shelters, increas-
ing the GNP, or arming everyone with a gun. The answer
lies with Jesus because *He alone can change the human heart.*

If the heart is not changed, then our institutions, values, and ways of judging reality will remain unchanged.
Conversion, *metanoia*, comes to all who dwell with Jesus
in spirit and truth. Conversion is the willingness to go and
see where Jesus dwells. Much to our surprise, we find He
dwells within us and desires to show us the way to the Father.

It is ultimately not to the hymn of Bernard but to the letter of the Apostle Paul to the Philippians that we turn for wisdom and hope.

> Have this mind among yourselves, which is yours in Christ Jesus, who, though he was in the form of God, did not count equality with God a thing to be grasped, but emptied himself, taking the form of a servant, being born in the likeness of men. And being found in human form he humbled himself and became obedient unto death, even death on a cross. Therefore God has highly exalted him and bestowed on him the name which is above every name, that at the name of Jesus every knee should bow, in heaven and on earth and under the earth, and every tongue confess that *Jesus Christ is Lord*, to the glory of God the Father. (Phil 2:5-11)

Jesus, who dwells with the Father *now*, dwells with us as one like us. Jesus speaks to the deepest desires of our heart and invites us to "come and see" so that we may be satisfied. Jesus comes as God's love letter with the message that through humble, suffering love there is exaltation; through obedience unto death there is the hope of eternal life; and through humiliation there is final vindication to the glory of the Father.

Our world is once again ready to hear the question of Jesus, "What do you seek?" We are called to be like Andrew and extend the invitation of Jesus anew: "Come and see." Our lives must proclaim the message of Andrew: "We have found the Messiah." The world must see in our hearts, our parishes, our homes, and our daily lives the indwelling of Jesus. Only then will others come and seek and stay with Jesus.

CHAPTER 2

'But who do you say that I am?' (Mt 16:15)

> When Jesus came to the neighborhood of Caesarea Philippi, he asked his disciples this question: "Who do people say the Son of Man is?" They replied. "Some say John the Baptizer, others Elijah, still others Jeremiah or one of the prophets." "And you," he said to them, "Who do you say that I am?" "You are the Messiah," Simon Peter answered, "the Son of the living God!" Jesus replied. "Blest are you, Simon Son of Jonah! No mere man has revealed this to you, but my heavenly Father. I for my part declare to you, you are 'Rock,' and on this rock I will build my church, and the jaws of death shall not prevail against it. I will entrust to you the keys of the kingdom of heaven. Whatever you declare bound on earth shall be bound in heaven; whatever you declare loosed on earth shall be loosed in heaven." (Matthew 16:13-19)

IN OUR FIRST chapter we encountered the fundamental question of human existence: What do you seek? This question of Jesus is directed to all men and women, and it demands a response. We indicated that many idols appear: power, money, popularity, pleasure, and sexuality. However, such idols fail to yield true happiness. Even with an abundance of idols, the human heart continues to search for that which gives lasting meaning and peace. The ultimate answer to the meaning of human existence is found by all who accept Jesus' invitation to "come and

see." It is Jesus alone who is able to give rest to our
hearts. Why? Because our hearts are made for God and
Jesus is *the* way to the Father. Jesus alone is the one who
can change hearts from stone to flesh.

We now turn our attention to the most fundamental
question asked by Jesus of the individual Christian and the
community as a whole. Jesus asks, "Who do you say that I
am?" We must not be too quick to answer. We must avoid
merely repeating answers from previous generations
without making the response truly our own. We must ar-
ticulate our own most personal answers to such questions
as: "Who is this Jesus we proclaim to be the one we seek,
follow, and long to stay with? How are we to understand
Jesus in light of the Cross and the hope of resurrection?
What is the meaning of Jesus for daily Christian witness?
How does the person of Jesus relate to the mission of the
Church?" As we can see, the questions of Jesus do not get
easier. They invite us to journey deeper and deeper into
the human condition and our relationship with Jesus. Such
a journey can be painful. Yet for those who allow themselves to be drawn into the questions of Jesus, eternal life
is theirs.

Ordinary experiences have a way of giving rise to extraordinary happenings. Jesus is traveling with His disciples to Caesarea Philippi. Matthew does not tell us what
occasioned Jesus' question, or what was so special about
that neighborhood (it is interesting to note that the contemporary British philosopher Bertrand Russell happened
upon some of his best insights while walking). Perhaps it
was just a case of curiosity on Jesus' part to see what others were saying about Him. The answers proceed: John
the Baptizer, Elijah, Jeremiah, or one of the prophets. The
answers are wrong. The question now becomes more personal and pointed toward the disciples themselves. Jesus
is no longer concerned about public opinion or the local

gossip. Jesus now wants to know what the disciples believe and know. Jesus asks, "Who do *you* say that I am?"

Simon Peter in one of his better moments (speaking under the influence — of inspiration, of course!) replies, "You are the Messiah, the Son of the living God!" To know Jesus as the Messiah is not something we earn or can demand because we do good works or belong to some elite religious group. To know Jesus is a *gift* from the Father to all who come searching for Jesus in truth. Jesus tells Peter, "Blest are you, Simon son of Jonah! No mere man has revealed this to you, but my heavenly Father."

Granted Peter proclaims Jesus as the Messiah and Son of God, we come to see how little he understands what he has said. Matthew's Gospel in the closing two sections (verses 21-23 and 24-28) indicates the shape of Jesus' Messiahship and the cost to one who follows Christ. Jesus must prepare "the little flock" for what is to come.

> From that time Jesus [the Messiah] began to show his disciples that he must go to Jerusalem and suffer many things from the elders, the chief priests and scribes, and be killed, and on the third day rise. (Mt 16:21)

These are chilling words. Anyone who doubts the realism of Jesus should weigh these words carefully. Jesus is the Messiah who must suffer, be rejected by all the respectable forces of the world, and endure a true, human death on the cross. The messiahship of Jesus is a scandal and stumbling block. In the words of Richard John Neuhaus, "the Lordship of Jesus is in constant dispute until he comes again in glory."

The shock value of Jesus' words do not take long in registering. Peter's notion of what a messiah should be and what Jesus is are in conflict. Peter says to Jesus, "May you be spared, Master! God forbid that any such thing ever happen to you!" Jesus, who just a few moments ago blessed Peter, declared him a rock-formation of His future church, and gave him the keys of authority, now turns on Peter and says. "Get behind me, Satan! You are a hindrance to me; for you are not on the side of God, but of men." The gesture by Peter seems so caring. Why should Jesus go to Jerusalem and certain death? Isn't Peter merely protecting his Master? We all know the connection between good intentions and disastrous results. Satan tries to use what is noble and caring and pervert it for his own destructive ends. We need only remember the words of St. Luke after recounting the three temptations of Jesus before the public ministry. "When the devil had finished all the tempting he left him, to await another opportunity" (Lk 4:13). Here is another opportunity. What could be more effective than protesting in the name of caring (remember the devil's temptations of materialism, power, and fame all failed) lest Jesus trip and fall?

This episode between Jesus and Peter is of timeless value. Regardless of our best intentions, we must come to accept Jesus as Messiah according to the will of the Father. The scandal and offense of the Cross cannot be bypassed or ignored. Our exaltation of Jesus only comes *after* Jesus is experienced as the Man of Sorrows. Jesus sits at the right hand of the Father *because* He has climbed upon the cross. Jesus is the Forsaken One who must "suffer many things from the elders, the chief priests and scribes, and be killed. . . ." Our doctrinal formulations, our daily spirituality, and celebrations of the Eucharist must always remain conscious of the Cross. Even the resurrected Lord appears with the marks of crucifixion. This is not morbid Christianity but the realism of God's love. In the words of St. Paul, "It is precisely in this that God proves his love for us: that while we were still sinners, Christ died for us" (Romans 5:8).

The implications of Jesus' Messiahship for the Christian life are crucial. There is no deceit in Jesus. Jesus

clearly indicates to the disciples what is required of one
who follows Him. "If any man would come after me, let
him deny himself and take up his cross and follow me."
We will explore these words of Jesus in greater detail in
the next chapter. Suffice it to say these words of self-denial are countercultural and offensive to an age that is
self-assertative and self-proclaiming. To an age that coun-
sels. "Pick up your pleasures," the challenge to "take up
the cross" is madness. Yet this is the way that leads to fellowship with Jesus.

Jesus asked His disciples who people believed the Son
of Man to be. There were a number of wrong answers in
the air. The question of Jesus — "Who do you say that I
am?" — is for us today. Answers abound: "Jesus is a
great moral teacher. Jesus is a radical who smashes the
idols of man-made religiosity. Jesus is a provider of en-
lightenment and divine truths." A popular image of Jesus
is one in which Jesus is accepted as Lord and Savior and
all our problems are solved. Also, books and articles are
written about Jesus "from below" and "from above."
That is, some emphasize the divinity of Jesus while others
center on His humanity. We could go on and on — the point
being that Jesus continues to fascinate us and the answers
about the identity continue to abound.

In terms of our *daily spirituality* — who is Jesus?
How can we come to know Jesus and be in fellowship with
Him? Jesus is the Messiah who suffers, dies, and rises
from the dead. *Jesus is the Messiah of the Paschal
Mystery*. It is through His death and resurrection that we
have the hope of eternal life in God. We come to know God
and be in fellowship with Jesus by being one with Jesus in
His Paschal Mystery, that is, by *our* daily dying and rising. We truly love Jesus to the extent that we turn our face
to Jerusalem, suffer rejection, experience death, and we
too shall be raised with Him. St. Thomas Aquinas in-

dicates there are two ways of knowing: first, knowing that perfects the self, and secondly, knowing that brings one in union with the one known. St. Thomas writes:

> There are two ways of desiring knowledge. One way is to desire it as a perfection of myself; and that is the way philosophers desire it. The other way of desiring knowledge is to desire it not [merely] as a perfection of myself, but because through this knowledge the one I love becomes present to me; and that is the way saints desire it.

We come to know *and* love Jesus (the way the saints desire it) by daily experiencing the Paschal Mystery. We are able to say with Simon Peter, "You are the Messiah, the Son of the living God."

To speak about our daily dying and rising with Jesus seems both abstract and a bit romantic. Few if any of us will be physically placed on a cross to die. Few if any of us will suffer persecution and find ourselves rejected by the forces of respectability for following Jesus. At the same time there is a romantic element about dying for what we believe in. The ability to suffer so others can live carries with it feelings of the "Impossible Dream." Martyrdom loses some of its gruesome qualities. However, our knowing and loving Jesus through the Paschal Mystery is at once concrete and filled with the hard realism of daily life.

How does the Paschal Mystery come to us in our daily lives?

How do we come to know Jesus as the Suffering Messiah through the particulars of our daily existences? Examples abound: the young person who struggles with doing what is right rather than what is easy; the Religious or priest who remains faithful to vows and commitments; the man or woman in the workplace who takes a stand for justice and the dignity of all persons over profits; and the elderly who continue to pray, sing, and be fully alive even though our Pepsi-Generation culture has declared them to be obsolete. All of these know the dying that is required. They also experience the rising to new life.

Being with Jesus and knowing Him through the Paschal Mystery has special meaning for husbands and wives and the life of the Church as a whole. Every truly living marriage requires a thousand and one daily dyings to self, egoism, pride, and one's own individual agenda. Dying is required to change one's vocabulary from "me, mine, and I" to "we, ours, and us." The Imperial Ego must make room for the other. Making room in our hearts for others is painful. Yet for those who do, the joy of the resurrection dawns. The sacrifices and daily journeys to Jerusalem are well worth the effort as one moves to new life in the New Jerusalem.

In the past two decades the Catholic Church has experienced profound changes. This has not always been easy. Much pain resulted and remains. For conservatives the Church moved too quickly. For liberals the Church has not moved quickly enough. Truth, like virtue, lies somewhere in the middle. One thing is for sure: *we must love this Church as she is today, and with hopeful confidence respond to the abiding Holy Spirit.* We are appreciative of our past and the richness of its heritage. We are hopeful of the Church's future, for Jesus promised to stay until the close of the age. In this present moment we love the Church. This means we must love and accept her as she is. This means at times we must die to our private agenda and individual dreams. We must blend our gifts and insights with the whole Body of Christ. At times we must be silent when we wish to speak, and speak when silence would be more comfortable. To be a living member of the Church means that we come to experience the deepest of Christian mysteries: that in dying we are reborn to eternal life. The whole life of the Church is one of telling the story of the Paschal Mystery. Who is Christ? The

Church answers by living the Paschal Mystery; that is, by dying daily with Christ so as to be reborn each day in His likeness. In the words of St. Paul:

> We were buried with him . . . by baptism into his death, so that as Christ was raised from the dead by the glory of the Father, we too might walk in newness of life. For if we have been united with him in a death like his, we shall certainly be united with him in a resurrection like his. (Rom 6:4-5)

The above-mentioned examples of daily dying with Jesus so as to share a like resurrection are by no means complete. We know only too well that in various parts of our world Christians continue to give the ultimate witness of faith — they surrender their lives so as to live a new way. Many of our brothers and sisters are physically jailed and abused for proclaiming Jesus is Lord. Many of our fellow pilgrims in faith are rejected by the powers of worldly respectability. They live as outcasts on the margins of society. For all of these, and for those whose daily dying is known to God alone, the question of Jesus ("Who do you say that I am?") and the doctrine of the Cross (the following of Jesus through self-denial) are real. The question of Jesus is not idle speculation but one of momentous importance. In our next chapter we shall explore further the implications of a Suffering Messiah and the cost of discipleship.

CHAPTER 3

'What profit does a man show who gains the whole world and destroys himself in the process?' (Mk 8:36)

> He summoned the crowd with his disciples and said to them: "If a man wishes to come after me, he must deny his very self, take up his cross, and follow in my steps. Whoever would preserve his life will lose it, but whoever loses his life for my sake and the gospel's will preserve it. What profit does a man show who gains the whole whorld and destroys himself in the process? What can a man offer in exchange for his life? If anyone in this faithless and corrupt age is ashamed of me and my doctrine, the Son of Man will be ashamed of him when he comes with the holy angels in his Father's glory." (Mark 8:34-38)

THE FIRST of Jesus' questions — What do you seek? — is one that raises the fundamental question of human existence. All people, because they are human, must offer a response. For the Christian the answer is Jesus. Our second chapter attempted to understand who Jesus is and what Jesus means for our spiritual life. We hold that Jesus is the Suffering Messiah who brings liberation and salvation through His Paschal Mystery of death and resurrection. The disciple is called to follow in Jesus' footsteps so as to experience a like resurrection. In this chapter we want to turn our attention to the issue of values; that is, the concrete life-style of the Christian. How does the Christian live so as to provide a daily witness to Jesus?

What values are at work in our lives if we profess to believe the Gospels? What is required of us on a daily basis so that we may (to paraphrase St. Richard of Chichester) know Jesus more clearly, love Him more dearly, and follow Him more nearly? To help us focus our reflections, we shall raise the question of Jesus contained in Mark's Gospel: "What profit does a man show who gains the whole world and destroys himself in the process?" or "What can a man offer in exchange for his life?"

The questions of Jesus are not rhetorical. They don't seek idle chatter or the multiplication of words which often conceal more than reveal. The questions of Jesus demand a response. The audiences for this question are fourfold: the crowd, the little flock of faith — the disciples — the community of Mark, and the generations of believers that will follow. The crowd represents those who are at the stage of inquiry or curiosity. They may have come to see what Jesus is all about, or they may have just happened accidentally to encounter Jesus. Jesus has just told the crowd what is required of staying with Him: "If a man wishes to come after me, he must deny his very self, take up his cross, and follow in my steps." In other words, to be in fellowship with Jesus requires that one leave boat, nets, former teachers, even family, and follow Him. No doubt many raised objections to such a radical demand. Worldly profits and obligations are attractive and pressing. Many in the crowd may have had a good business, long-standing family connections, and legitimate concerns of home and family. Yet Jesus clearly indicates that none of these are of gain *if* they take precedence over Jesus and the Gospel. Worldly concerns and achievements have a way of blinding us to our true destiny — life with God. We come to believe that we are more because we possess more. The abundance of our goods becomes equated with our personal goodness. We are rich because we deserve to be so. This is a sign of God's love. The poor and suffering are only paying for their sins. Jesus rejects such faulty reasoning. True riches are not the abundance of our bank accounts but the degree to which we follow Jesus. We know from reading the Gospels that many could not accept this teaching. The clearest example is contained in the Gospel of Mark (10:17-27).

A rich man comes to Jesus seeking the conditions for discipleship. The man has kept the commandments. He is a good man. Mark tells us Jesus "looked at him with love." Then came the invitation to radical discipleship. "There is one more thing you must do. Go and sell what you have and give to the poor; you will then have treasure in heaven. After that, come and follow me." Mark goes on to indicate that the outcome was not a joyful one. The man was still married to his earthly possessions. "He went away sad, for he had many possessions." Once again we see that the demands of discipleship do not allow us to hug the middle and seek the comfortable compromise. Only one master may be served.

The question of Jesus — what can one offer in exchange for life? — is also for the Twelve who travel with him. They have left home, family, business, and daily occupation. New friends, values, and a way of life have been embraced. The Twelve have accepted the radical demands that go with the invitation to follow Jesus. The Twelve have been generous. Peter (ever the one to speak up) is not bashful about reminding Jesus of the cost: "We have put aside everything to follow you!" (Mk 10:28). Jesus takes up Peter's challenge. Human generosity is never greater than God's favor. Human generosity is always a *response* to the gracious God who first gave to us and loved us. Human generosity never occasions God's love but is always a recognition of what God first did for us and what we are to do for one another. Hence Jesus responds: "I give you my word, there is no one who has left house or brothers or sisters or mother or father or children or lands, for my sake and for the gospel, who will not receive a hundredfold now in this time, houses and brothers and sisters and mothers and children and lands, with persecutions, and in the age to come eternal life" (Mk 10:29-30).

Two things are worthy of our attention in Jesus' response. First we should note that God's generosity is not part of some divine layaway plan. God's generosity is for the *present* age. In the here and now we are to experience God's love. The following of Jesus is not delayed gratification. In following Jesus totally, we come to experience a joy which no one can take from us. The happiness we experience on earth is but a shadow of the joy we shall know when we see Jesus face to face. Second, Jesus and Mark, ever the realists, remind us that along with the generosity of God, the disciple must contend with the hostility of the world. Jesus says that along with the hundredfold of good things there will be also "persecutions." The disciples have given up their whole world in order to follow Jesus. They are willing to lose their lives for Jesus and the Gospel. All this they have done because they know (however imperfectly) and believe (however weakly) that in Jesus they have found the One who gives life in abundance.

The third audience addressed by the question of Jesus is Mark's own community. Mark's Gospel is written between A.D. 67 and 70. The chief source of Mark's material is the preaching of Peter. Mark's community consists mainly of non-Palestinian Christians of pagan origin. Hence we notice that Mark makes little connection between the Old Testament and the Gospel. Mark goes to great lengths to explain various Jewish customs. Mark above all wants to explain the meaning of the Gospel for pagans. Against this background Mark is given a tough task: proclaim the Crucified Jesus as the Messiah and Son of God. Jesus is not a political leader who uses forces to achieve his end. Rather, it is through suffering love that the kingdom has broken into history. The climax of Mark's Gospel is reached in chapter fifteen with the confession of the centurion: "Truly this man was the Son of God!" (15:39). In irony more typical of John's Gospel, we find the true identity of Jesus proceeding from the lips of the hated Gentile — a Roman soldier. Indeed Jesus is the Messiah who must suffer and die. This is the secret that cannot be told ahead of time. One must relinquish all that one holds and follow Jesus. Only then can one proclaim Jesus as Messiah.

Mark's community has experienced tough times; persecution and discrimination are not uncommon. Some are beginning to question the wisdom of following Jesus. After all, He is a Messiah who reigns from a cross. The community has its own question: Is the following of Jesus worth all the suffering it is enduring? The answer by Mark is clear: Yes. Hold on and keep the faith. God was able to take the hostility of the world directed toward Jesus and transform it for salvation. God will do the same thing for the community of faith. Persecutions are to be expected, but don't despair. The hostility of worldly powers will be used by God to strengthen the community. The blood of the martyrs helps the Church to grow. I don't think it is by accident that Mark closes chapter eight with the Suffering Messiah and opens chapter nine with the Transfiguration. The Messiah who must suffer, be rejected, and die is also the one who stands between Moses and Elijah. The Suffering Messiah completes the law and the prophets. Israel's history is completed in the person of Jesus and the Cross. The Crucified One is also the Transfigured and Resurrected One. Both aspects of Jesus must be embraced — the cross and the empty tomb. Mark is encouraging his com-

munity to endure the present trials with resolute faith and
the hope of new life.

Finally, Mark's gospel and the question of Jesus —
what can one offer in exchange for life? — are for us. The
question of Jesus does not afford us the luxury of simply
repeating the past in a way that is not our own. The question of Jesus demands that *we* hear the question anew and
formulate an answer which proceeds from our situation
today. We may no longer seek more fish, bigger boats, or
full nets. Today we want a big bank account, the summer
home, or 1,001 other idols that clutter up our own faithless
and corrupt age (evidently we do not have a monopoly on
evil). Today we may suffer persecution in a different way.
It is not the suffering of guns and physical death but the
suffering of indifference and a spiritual death that we
often experience. We feel a little uneasy speaking about
Jesus and His meaning for our life. After all, we do not
want to offend those who believe differently, or do not believe at all. We become tolerant to the point of being non-
commital. Is not much of this uneasiness part of our being
ashamed of Jesus and the Gospel?

The question of Jesus — what does it profit one to gain
the whole world and yet lose life? — has special cash value
for us. This question of Jesus is really the question of commitment. Jesus is asking the following: To what or to
whom are you committed? In what or in whom have you
placed your hope for life? This question of Jesus is so important and difficult because it requires that we make a
commitment. If there is one thing we moderns try to avoid
at all cost it is commitment and promise-making. The
word commitment is a fear word. At its mention the
palms get moist, the brow accumulates sweat, the stom-
ach dances, and the throat is filled with a baseball.

Unfortunately, we have come to understand commitment as that which threatens our freedom. To commit

ourselves to something larger than the self is viewed today as slavery. We are told we must keep our options open and play it cool. We must march to our own music and be our own drummer. Yet, in our more reflective moments, we come to realize that authentic freedom is always expressed through commitment. It is only when we forget ourselves, transcend ourselves, deny ourselves, and donate ourselves that we become truly human, free, and loving. Commitment is for the mature. Only those who have a strong sense of self-identity and self-esteem are able to risk involvement with others and just causes.

Today we witness such a fear of commitment. This is especially true when it comes to marriage and religious-vocation promises. We wonder, and not without good reason, if we can say yes to God and another person forever. We are fearful of making promises that demand of us an involvement beyond the moment. Young people preparing for marriage often ask if they can say yes to loving each other for today and all the days God gives them. Young people preparing for religious commitment search their hearts to see if they can promise themselves to God forever. In a world of rapid change and short-term encounters, these concerns are real. Too often the creases in our pants and skirts last longer than our promises and vows. It is not uncommon today to find people making radical life-style and commitment changes after many years. It is not for us to judge such changes. However, the questions raised by such changes are of concern.

Father Karl Rahner, S.J., in a beautiful essay titled "Vocation," reminds us that *"The courage of irreversible decisions is something that belongs necessarily to the essence of the true and valiant human being."* In freedom and uncertainty we make such commitments. We do not receive special-delivery letters from heaven telling us what to do and become in clear and dis-

tinct ways. Life is risky business. There are no private
revelations telling us exactly what to do. We are free and
we must discern God's dream for our lives. But as Father
Rahner goes on to say, one must "live today in such a way
that you will be able to carry out this priestly office and its
obligations tomorrow as well. In a sense, you need not
make decisions and dispositions now for when you are
forty. But you can live and act now in such a way that, as
far as lies within your freedom, you will still be able to be
an honest and enthusiastic priest when you are forty."
Naturally we can apply Father Rahner's works to the
married and single states as well. In effect, by daily deny-
ing the self, taking up the cross, and following Christ, we
have the reasonable hope of fidelity to our irreversible decisions. It is in risking and losing our lives for the sake of
Jesus and the Gospel that we truly live.

The question of Jesus invites us to make the most important commitments of our lives. What are those things,
persons, and events which we consider profit? What are
the innumerable daily ways in which we have been challenged to die to ourselves and live for Christ? What little
exchanges have we made in place of the life offered by
Jesus? In what ways have we been ashamed of Jesus and
the Gospel? Such questions are not merely asked in order
to fill up the time. They touch on our fundamental relationship with Jesus. The answers we give are drawn from our
daily witness.

Commitment to Jesus and the Gospel is never easy or
selective. Through the Incarnation, God has given Himself
completely to us. The call and the cost of discipleship require that we follow Jesus in the greatness of His preaching and the awe-inspiring doing of His miracles. We are to
be with Jesus during the multiplication of loaves and fish-
es, the curing of the sick, the expulsion of demons, and the

raising of the dead. We are also required to be in fellowship with Jesus in His time of rejection, hostility, and hatred. We must walk with Jesus toward Jerusalem. The next question that claims our attention concerns our ability to keep fellowship with Jesus in His suffering.

CHAPTER 4

'Could you not watch one hour?' (Mk 14:37)

They went then to a place named Gethsemane. "Sit down here while I pray," he [Jesus] said to his disciples; at the same time he took along with him Peter, James, and John. Then he began to be filled with fear and distress. He said to them, "My heart is filled with sorrow to the point of death. Remain here and stay awake." He advanced a little and fell to the ground, praying that if it were possible this hour might pass him by. He kept saying, "*Abba* (O Father), you have the power to do all things. Take this cup away from me. But let it be as you would have it, not as I." When he returned he found them asleep. He said to Peter. "Asleep, Simon? You could not stay awake for even an hour? Be on guard and pray that you may not be put to the test. The spirit is willing but nature is weak." (Mark 14:32-38)

ST. MARK paints a picture of a troubled Jesus; and one which troubles us. Jesus is about to reach the climax of His mission. The last meal has been shared. Yet instead of joy and anticipation, we find talk of betrayal and denial. The garden scene is not one of fulfillment but one of dread. The depression is so great that the disciples seek release in sleep. St. Mark tells us that Jesus is filled with fear and distress. His heart runs over with a sorrow to the point of death. Jesus prays that His Father will remove the cup He was sent to drink. Jesus does not even enjoy the comfort and support of His disciples. St.Mark tells us in words that are brutally honest: "Their eyes were very heavy; and they did not know what to answer him" (Mk 14:40). Is this the Messiah? Can this truly be the Son of God and the hope of Israel? Is this testimony by St. Mark not a scandal and a cause for defection? Will not these few verses shake the faith of little ones?

The answer offered by St. Mark to all of these questions is "Yes." Yes, Jesus is the Messiah, Son of God, and the hope of Israel. The Messiah who suffers is a scandal and will cause many to turn away. The faith of little ones will be tested in the Garden and at Golgotha. Yet this picture of Jesus must be painted, and this testimony of faith must be shared. Why? St. Mark wants us to appreciate and love Jesus in His humanity. What St. Mark offers here and throughout his Gospel is a very human Jesus. Jesus grows weary, is hungry, needs rest, and at times needs to be far away from the crowds. The Fourth Gospel tells us that "the Word became flesh" (Jn 1:14). St. Mark shows us how completely human the Word became — totally human. This human Jesus has always proved troubling to the Church. Even the Gospel writers have had the need to elevate the status of Jesus. For example, while St. Luke (22:39-46) mentions the anguish of Jesus to the degree that "his sweat became like great drops of blood," Luke does not mention Jesus being overcome with fear, distress, and a heart that is filled with sorrow to the point of death. Also we notice the sleeping of the disciples receives less treatment. And finally, St. Luke adds the presence of an angel who "appeared to him . . . from heaven, strengthening him." The Gospel of John goes even further by eliminating the agony in the Garden altogether. Following the Great Discourses (chapters 14-17), John has Jesus arrested but not before claiming His divinity: "When he said to them, 'I am he,' they drew back and fell to the ground" (Jn 18:6). John wants his readers to know that Jesus is I AM. Jesus is Yahweh with a human face. As with Moses, so it is with the guards who arrest Jesus; in the presence of God, one must fall to the ground.

What about the disciples? How could they have been so insensitive and ungrateful? After all that Jesus had done for them and taught them, you would think they could be with Jesus in His hour of need. Yet the synoptic writers tell us that the disciples could not remain awake for even an hour. Before we get too carried away in our judgments, let us temper our harshness with the realization that we are 2,000 years removed and secure in our homes. It is too easy to look back in anger or bewilderment at the actions of a past generation. In time, however, we will be someone's past. Let us try to move from condemnation to reconciliation; from heat to light, so as better to appreciate the disciples' situation. In so doing we may better understand ourselves.

Why did the disciples fall asleep? Maybe it was the lateness of the hour. Maybe the dinner was too heavy. Maybe the day's work had been too hard and sleep was too strong to delay. Mark and Luke provide a different explanation. Mark indicates that the disciples could not stay awake and they "did not know what to answer him." The disciples were incapable of offering Jesus comfort and support. They were inadequate to the task. Luke is even more explicit. He indicates that Jesus finds the disciples asleep, exhausted with grief (22:45). Jesus is about to be handed over to the forces of darkness. What Peter had hoped to spare Jesus was about to take place. The disciples were so depressed and filled with uncertainty that they sought safety in sleep.

If Mark presents Jesus in human terms, the disciples are no less human. The disciples are limited, weak, dull, and prone to pettiness. In short, Jesus has not selected saints, supermen, or mythical figures to be His followers. The Word made flesh has chosen real human beings with

all of the contradictions and limitations of the weak flesh,
our human nature. Mark's description of Jesus' disciples
not knowing what to say to Him is so human. Many a
priest, relative, and friend of a suffering and dying person
feels similarly inadequate. Words are so limited. We do
not know what to say or to do. We feel the utter futility of
the situation. *All* we can do is be present. *All* we can do is
be with the suffering and dying one in holy silence. Yet we
feel that we must say or do something. We also know that
we too want to avoid such situations. We do not talk about
it. We change the subject, hoping all will go away. When
we cannot avoid suffering and death any longer, we can
fall into a depression. Many a hospital room is filled with
the bodies of loved ones who are "exhausted with grief."
The research of Doctor Elisabeth Kübler-Ross indicates
that depression is one of the stages in the dying process on
the way to acceptance and hope. St. Matthew, in his account of the agony in the garden, has Jesus saying, "Sleep
on now. Enjoy your rest! The hour is on us when the Son of
Man is to be handed over to the power of the evil men"
(26:45). Jesus even to the end is the Man for others. Jesus
recognizes the weakness of the human condition. There
are no words of condemnation. Once again Jesus is trying
to prepare the disciples for what is to come.

Once again, the question of Jesus is for us: "You could
not stay awake for even an hour?" If we are honest with
ourselves our response to keeping fellowship with Jesus in
the garden may not be all that different from the disciples'. What words would we say to Jesus? What comfort
would we offer? How would we be supportive of the One
who seemed to carry the burdens of others? Let us not be
too quick to give an answer or an offer of support. We need
only remember the example of Peter recorded in Scripture. Just before St. Mark records the agony in the Garden
we are presented with Jesus predicting Peter's denial.

Jesus tells the disciples their faith in Him will be shaken. Peter protests. "Even though they all fall away, I will not." No doubt Peter is sincere. However, more than sincerity is required. Jesus indicates that Peter will deny Him three times (more will be said about this in our next chapter). Peter continues to proclaim his fidelity. " 'Even if I must die with you, I will not deny you.' And they all said the same." (Mk 14:31). One day Peter's words will come true. He will die for love of Jesus. On this night, however, "the sheep will be scattered."

To the question of Jesus — you could not stay awake for even an hour? — we must answer with questions of our own: Why should we be in fellowship with Jesus in His suffering? Why is it important for us to stay awake? Why should we not enjoy the escape offered by sleep as the darkness of the next three days unfolds? These are not flippant questions but very human ones. Let us venture two responses for our keeping fellowship with Jesus in His agony.

On the most basic level, we human beings belong to one another and are important for one another. Human existence is shared existence. We need and depend on one another for survival and growth. Life is connected. We are not meant to be islands separated from one another in less than grand isolation. The actions of one affect the well-being of all. Authentic human existence is being with and for the other as much as we are for ourselves. Jesus is a member of the human family and is in need of human comfort and support. Jesus needs the fellowship of His disciples so that *He* can be strengthened for the trial. Once again, those who work with the dying know the importance of physical presence and support. The greatest fear of the dying is not pain but loneliness. To die alone is a terrible thing. Granted, no one can die our death. Yet we need to experience fellowship with others, the presence of our fellow human beings. In moments of sickness and dying, we need to know we are still loved and cared for. St. Mark presents the human Jesus in need of human fellowship. We need to stay with Jesus in His suffering so that we can experience what God is about. God is love, and in Jesus we come to see that love is the willingness to make a total commitment. Love calls on us to suffer for the other and even be willing to make the ultimate sacrifice. To be one with Jesus in the garden is to experience how much we are loved by God and how much we are to love in return. In the end, it is not we who have to say anything. It is Jesus who speaks to us: "Watch and stay with me. Keep fellowship with me and share my cup. Be baptized with the fire of my baptism. Stay with me and experience the depth of the Divine Love. Pray that you may be able to accept your cross as it comes. In watching with me in my suffering, you shall be one with me in the resurrection."

Our second response concerns the moments in our life when we are broken and suffering. In the moments of our personal Gethsemane, how do we respond? We can rebel and rage against the dying of the light. We can shake our fist at God or the unfeeling cosmos and curse the day we were born. We can withdraw from others and become a prisoner in our pain. We can accept our pain and suffering with the indifference of the stoic. We remain unmoved. Suffering is endured with a fatalistic silence that gives evidence of a hopeless spirit. We simply wait for the end. There is a third way — the way of Jesus.

The Christian in fellowship with the suffering Jesus does not rebel or despair. Rather, the Christian searches for *meaning* in suffering. Suffering reminds us that we are limited, fragile, finite, and terminal. Suffering challenges our feelings of self-sufficiency and autonomy. We can be hurt. Suffering above all challenges us to broaden our horizons and consider the things that really matter.

Suffering reminds us to look beyond the glories of this world and consider eternity. Suffering reminds us of the "other dimension" of existence in which we stand before God. Suffering can only be understood in this way when we keep fellowship with Jesus in His agony.

Jesus does not eliminate our suffering but transforms and elevates its meaning. This is crucial to remember. The Christian is not excused from involvement with the concerns of daily life. Involvement means risk, and risk demands faith. Only those who truly love will suffer. Only those who keep fellowship with Jesus are able to bring comfort to the afflicted. This is the great mystery of human suffering from the perspective of the Christian story. St. Paul, writing to the Colossians, says: "Now I rejoice in my sufferings for your sake, and in my flesh I complete what is lacking in Christ's afflictions for the sake of his body, that is, the church" (Col 1:24). How can Paul, and all Christians, rejoice in suffering? Isn't this attitude a sick one? Perhaps, to the standards of the world, but to faith it is the way to salvation. Paul sees *through* the Cross of the risen Christ. Paul can be a man of joy in all circumstances because the goal of his life is Christ.

St. Paul goes further by claiming something quite shocking: he and the community complete the sufferings of Christ. Paul does not mean that we perfect the sacrifice of Jesus. The cross of Jesus is the perfect sacrifice once and for all. Yet each of us in his own way carries Christ to the world in our daily sufferings. In our moments of betrayal, denial, loneliness, sickness of the spirit, sadness of heart, and when our sweat becomes like blood, we are to be one with Christ. We too are to drink that cup and do the will of the Father. In all of our personal nights in Gethsemane, when all have forsaken us, we commend all to the loving arms of God. For it is only through the transforming power of love that we can move beyond

Gethsemane and travel the road to Emmaus. Only through love, in the midst of darkness and death, can our eyes be opened and our hearts set burning inside (see Lk 24:13-29).

To be in fellowship with Jesus in suffering is still a question for Christian and Church. Jesus continues to ask: "You could not stay awake for even an hour?" As the poor man Lazarus continues to be ignored outside the rich man's house, so Jesus continues to be at Gethsemane and in need of fellowship. Where is Jesus in His need to be found? Jesus is where He has always been: in the hungry, the thirsty, the stranger, the naked, the ill, and those in captivity (see Mt 25:31-46). We are called to be in solidarity with our brothers and sisters in need. In so doing, we minister to Christ in His need. Jesuit theologian René Latourelle expresses the need to be in fellowship with Jesus and others in the following way:

> Salvation has to be proclaimed yesterday, today and tomorrow; it has to be proclaimed not only in words but in deeds. . . . We must make Christ "visible" in his decisive action, in his gift-of-self-to-others. But it is through our suffering, when this is linked to the suffering of Christ, that we so resemble Christ in his redemptive act that we become his living, present witnesses; we represent Christ as handed over, given for all. *(Man and His Problems in the Light of Jesus Christ)*

CHAPTER 5

'Simon, Son of John, do you love me?'

(Jn 21:17)

> When they had finished breakfast, Jesus said to Simon
> Peter, "Simon, son of John, do you love me more than
> these?" He said to him, "Yes, Lord; you know that I love
> you." [Jesus] said to him, "Feed my lambs." A second
> time he said to him, "Simon, son of John, do you love me?"
> [Peter] said to him, "Yes, Lord; you know that I love you."
> He said to him, "Tend my sheep." He said to him the third
> time, "Simon, son of John, do you love me?" Peter was
> grieved because he said to him the third time, "Do you love
> me?" And he said to him, "Lord, you know everything; you
> know that I love you." Jesus said to him, "Feed my
> sheep." (John 21:15-17).

REGARDLESS of how one approaches the Gospels — as
friend or foe, skeptic or believer — one thing is im-
pressively clear: the writers of the Gospels are not involved in a cover-up. The Gospel writers, and for that matter the writers of Scriptures as a whole, present real human beings in all of their complexities. In the Old Testament, for example, we have recorded the heroism and
faltering of Moses. The innocence of David as well as his
sins are clearly before us. The New Testament is no different. The weakness of the disciples is not passed over.
Among the Twelve are found one who denies, one who be-
trays, and all forsake Jesus. The various conflicts that

beset the early Church are recorded in the various New-
Testament writings. A good example is contained in the
Acts of the Apostles. In chapter two St. Luke tells us the
new community members "devoted themselves to the
apostles' teaching and fellowship, to the breaking of bread
and the prayers" (Acts 2:42). This highly complimentary
picture is balanced by the conflict in chapter fifteen of
Acts. Some leading members of the community want to
impose Jewish laws on Gentile converts to Christianity.
Probably the first Church council is convened. Paul rejects such requirements. Salvation is only through faith in
Jesus Christ. St. Luke does not try to cover up early controversies. They are part of the record. In fact, such conflicts are to be expected from any community which takes
seriously the invitation to follow Jesus.

All of the above is said to order to help us appreciate
the stories of faith and the portraits of men and women
wrestling with the Lord. The weakness of individual faith
and the narrowness of community vision ought not to turn
us off. Rather, we should be turned on to God's unbounded
love. God doesn't love us and reveal Himself to us because
we are perfect. God doesn't raise up leaders because they
never make mistakes, grow weary, or sin. In reading the
Bible we find that the so-called heroes of faith are made of
clay. Too often we want heroes and leaders and Messiahs
who are everything but human. Yet the testimony of Scripture will not allow us this luxury. Jesus is truly human,
and yet the Messiah who is rejected and put to death. The
Apostle Paul beautifully expresses the limits and greatness of a human, Christian life:

> But we have this treasure in earthen vessels, to show that
> the transcendant power belongs to God and not to us. We
> are afflicted in every way, but not crushed; perplexed, but
> not driven to despair; persecuted, but not forsaken; struck
> down, but not destroyed; always carrying in the body the

death of Jesus, so that the life of Jesus may be manifested
in our mortal flesh. (2 Cor 4:7-10)

Let us turn our attention to the question of Jesus —
"Do you love me?" We want to reflect on what it means to
love Jesus. Also we want to know Peter's life can help us
love Jesus more clearly. Of interest as well is the brief
question-and-answer exchange between Peter and Jesus
for Church leadership. And finally, we want to reflect on
the story of God that emerges as Peter passes from denial
to affirmation; from weeping bitterly to confident love.

If the word commitment fills us with fear, then the
word love fills us with confusion. In the modern context,
love has fallen victim to what logicians call "over-ex-
tension." That is, the word love has been overworked and
exhausted. It has been used so much that it has fallen into
misuse and abuse. We love our cars, animals, hobbies,
friends, and spouses. We love our favorite foods and favorite forms of entertainment. We confuse love with lust, and
intimacy with exploitation or vulgar exposure. Simply
put: in the modern context, love is suffering from a severe
identity crisis. Hence, if we are to speak about loving
Jesus, we ought to be clear about what it means to say, "I
love."

Love is the most basic human vocation. We are made
to love and be loved. Love is our destiny or the fulfillment
of our humanity. We are most truly human when we love
and accept love. Love is always a risk. Love makes us into
a zone of uncertainty in which our most basic instrument
is trust. There are no guarantees about the outcome of
love and risk-taking. We can lose in the game of love. Yet
if defeat is not to be lasting, we must continue to risk and
trust and hope. To allow ourselve to be lastingly defeated
in love is the ultimate sin. Sin is so repulsive because it
distorts our nature. Sin is our free refusal to be open to the
unbounded demands of love. We may commit many sins,

but they all return to the one source of sin — the refusal to love enough. The power of love is the highest expression of our freedom. Love calls our freedom to reality by inviting us to come out of ourselves for the one who needs us in the concrete situation. In other words, love is a verb. Love is active and involves us in doing more than feeling. Contrary to the conventional wisdom, love often requires that we transcend our feelings and move beyond them. This is not a denial of feelings, but the wisdom that loving requires more than feelings. Love involves the whole acting person: feelings, intellect, memory, imagination, and a free decision of the will.

Lest all this talk about love seem too abstract and disembodied (this is always a danger), let us reflect on the various commitments (that word again) that make up our daily existence. Husbands and wives know that love requires self-donation and transcending the imperial self. In spite of feelings of resentment, hurt, indifference, and anger, love endures and the covenant grows. Religious and priests know the feelings of disappointment, despair, and fear that what one does matters little. Yet, against all such feelings, these men and women continue to proclaim Christ crucified and risen. Every good friendship requires that we move beyond feelings of being taken for granted, being overlooked, and not having one's concerns taken seriously. Friends know that love heals the wounds of such hurts. Finally, we can reflect on the work in which we are engaged. At times every work becomes boring, tiring, trivial, and alienating. Yet we continue to dedicate ourselves to its demands. We do so because these negative feelings cannot compare to the overall payoff of a work we love. In all of these and many other ways, love moves us beyond the feelings of the moment. We accept the long view.

With the above in mind, we can ask: What does it

mean to love Jesus? First and foremost, we must remember that loving Jesus is a *response* to His first loving
us. The first letter of John puts it this way: "We love, because he first loved us" (1 Jn 4:19). Again John writes:
"In this is love: not that we loved God but that he loved us
and sent his Son to be an expiation for our sins" (1 Jn
4:10). Jesus came and showed us what it means to truly
love God and others. Love is laying down one's life for the
other. We do not earn God's love. God's love is a free gift
to us. God first loved us because God is love and not because we have a just claim to that love. In fact, God loved
us when we were most powerless — under the power of sin
and death. Paul writes to the Romans: "God shows his
love for us in that while we were yet sinners Christ died
for us" (Rom 5:8).

   Second, to authentically love Jesus means that we love
Jesus in His totality and not some part we have fashioned.
Love is the total surrender to the total person and message
of Jesus. We cannot love only the Jesus who gives the keys
of the Kingdom without also loving the Jesus who turns
His face to Jerusalem. We cannot follow the Jesus who
cures and forgives sins if we are not prepared to follow
Him to Golgotha. In other words, we can fall in love with
some romantic *idea* of Jesus. This is not love but senti-
ment. To romanticize about Jesus is to deny the Jesus of
the Incarnation — to love the Word *without* flesh. Love is
the total acceptance of what one is totally. To the question
of Jesus — "Do you love me?" — we answer yes if we can
say yes to the Word made flesh, the Suffering Messiah, the
Man of Sorrows, the Abandoned One of God, the Risen
Lord, the Son who sits at the right hand of the Father, and
the One who will come in glory. True love of Jesus requires that we say yes to *all* of this. Anything less is not a
true love of Jesus.

   A troubling question arises: Granted we know what it

means to love Jesus, can we love Jesus today when we are so far removed from Him in terms of culture and history? Do not 2,000 years and geo-cultural factors negate our loving the authentic Jesus? These are serious questions. Let us say that love carries us beyond the transcends these barriers. We can love Jesus today and tomorrow because He lives! Yes, Jesus, crucified and laid to rest in the tomb, is alive. Jesus does not abandon us but sends another Paraclete, the Holy Spirit, to dwell in our hearts. Jesus *has* returned with the coming of the Paraclete at Pentecost. Jesus *will* come in the fullness of glory at the end of time. The indwelling of the Spirit liberates us to respond in love to the One who loved us to the end and to a new beginning.

The mystery of the Incarnation continues to unfold. We can love Jesus today by loving our neighbor today. Each time we meet the needs of another we love Jesus. Each time we give water, food, clothing, a sheltering welcome, and extend a kindness to those who know so little kindness, we minister to Jesus in His needs. We transcend the barriers of space and time. We may not do this consciously. We may not see Jesus directly in the poor, the hungry and those on the margins of our society. We may only "see" a human being in need. Yet the result is the same: in doing love to one of these we do love to Jesus.

What can we learn from Peter's life that will help us to love Jesus more dearly? Peter's relationship with Jesus teaches us the importance of patience and discipline. This is no small lesson in a world that courts the quick fix and the instant gratification. Our love relationship with Jesus takes time. There are no techniques, courses, magic formulas, or even books that can promise one instant of intimacy with Jesus. Relationships, if they are to grow and be healthy, require patience, and patience requires discipline. Patience is essential for intimacy. We cannot punch up the spiritual card on the computer and be turned on to

Jesus. We must be willing to travel with Jesus in the daily contours of our existence. This means we must not despair over our failures, denials, and betrayals. Also we must not become boastful over our advances in the spiritual life. Peter's life is anything but the upward line of progress. Peter has his moments of greatness (in Matthew, chapter 16) and his moments of weakness (John, chapter 18). In our failures we turn to Jesus for reconciliation. In our successes we turn to Jesus in gratitude. Through patience we win our lives and grow in loving Jesus. Peter proclaimed Jesus the Messiah and was given the keys of the kingdom. Peter was denounced by Jesus as speaking the words of Satan. Peter tells Jesus all may betray Him but he never will. Peter denies the Lord three times. Peter affirms his love for Jesus three times. Which is the real Peter? Much to our dislike, we must say *all* of these. We may prefer "a clear and distinct" Peter, but there is none in the offing. Peter is complex. So are we.

The Fourth Gospel contains many dialogues between Jesus and various individuals or groups (Nicodemus in chapter 3; the Samaritan woman in chapter 4; confrontation between Jesus and the authorities over the man born blind in chapter 9). The reading from the Fourth Gospel which opened this chapter contains a brief dialogue between Jesus and Peter. In the dialogue we hear the three denials become the three affirmations of love by Peter. This dialogue is also crucial for Church and parish leadership.

Jesus invites Peter to proclaim his love. After Peter does so, Jesus indicates how love for Jesus will be shown: "Feed my lambs." Peter is to be a good shepherd in the likeness of the One who is the Good Shepherd. Leadership involves nourishment. The community is to be nourished by word and deed so as to follow Jesus. Leadership never seeks its own praise but always the glory of God through

Jesus in the Paraclete. The heart of community life is fellowship with Jesus Christ crucified and risen.

Jesus indicates to Peter that the members of the community belong to Him: "Feed *my* sheep." Inauthentic leadership tries to take the place of Jesus and become the center of community life. The Christian community must be on constant vigil against the rise of "personality-cult religion." We do not follow Reverend Jones or Father Smith. We follow Jesus. The role of the leader is one of stewardship and trust. Leadership is empowered and entrusted with the well-being of the community. How well this stewardship is exercised is the degree to which the community grows in loving Jesus and one another. Leaders are crucially important but not ultimately important. Leaders are never the end but always a means to Jesus. The goal is always life in Jesus.

Above all leadership requires the willingness to pay the ultimate price — to give one's life out of love. After the third affirmation of love, Jesus indicates to Peter what it means to nourish the community:

> Truly, truly, I say to you, when you were young, you girded yourself and walked where you would; but when you are old, you will stretch out your hands, and another will gird you and carry you where you do not wish to go. (Jn 21:18)

John tells us that Jesus said these words to indicate that Peter would be killed for the glory of God. These few lines are a sobering reminder to all who are leaders in the Christian community. To follow Jesus is to drink the cup and be baptized in the fire of the Cross. Leaders in loving Jesus must be among the first to arrive in Jerusalem!

Finally, as mentioned earlier, we see the denials of Peter become the affirmations of love for Jesus. Jesus does not offer angry words of condemnation, nor is Peter removed from his leadership position. Rather, Jesus invites Peter to make a mature, seasoned commitment to

Him. Jesus has prayed that Peter would survive the trial
and emerge stronger in faith and love. The bitter tears of
repentance must move to the challenges of leading this
fragile, new community. Repentance must not become
self-pity or despair. Jesus asks simply: "Do you love
me?"

The story of God (to use Father John Shea's phrase)
that emerges is important for us. Jesus comes to tell us of
the Father's unbounded love. Jesus comes out of love and
to liberate us for love. The power of sin and death will not
have the final word in God's creation. Love is the power to
heal the past and open up a future that is hopeful. The denials of Peter and the betrayal of Judas are not foreign to
us. We have our own price for selling Jesus and our own
form of declaring, "I do not know the man!" The response
of Judas was despair and suicide. The response of Peter
was contrition, reconciliation, and hope. Past failure did
not destroy present and future possibilities for love and
life. Peter fell, but he also rose through and into the love of
the One who is life in abundance.

So it is with us. What are the ways in which we have
denied and betrayed Jesus? How have we been tempted to
despair of reconciliation? Peter stands as a reminder that
there is a better way. Peter reminds us that we can move
from denial to affirmation; from despair to hope; and
from death to life. It is up to us. It all depends on how we
answer the question of Jesus: "Do you love me?"

PART II

Loving the Neighbor

CHAPTER 6

'Which of these three, do you think, proved neighbor to the man who fell among the robbers?' (Lk 10:36)

And behold a lawyer stood up to put him to the test, saying "Teacher, what shall I do to inherit eternal life?" [Jesus] said to him, "What is written in the law? How do you read?" And he answered, "You shall love the Lord your God with all your heart, and with all your soul, and with all your strength, and with all your mind; and your neighbor as yourself." And he said to him, "You have answered right; do this and you will live." But he, desiring to justify himself, said to Jesus, "And who is my neighbor?" Jesus replied, "A man was going down from Jerusalem to Jericho, and he fell among robbers, who stripped him and beat him, and departed, leaving him half dead. Now by chance a priest was going down that road; and when he saw him he passed by on the other side. So likewise a Levite, when he came to the place and saw him, passed by on the other side. But a Samaritan, as he journeyed, came to where he was; and when he saw him, he had compassion, and went to him on his own beast and brought him to an inn, and took care of him. And the next day he took out two denarii and gave them to the innkeeper, saying, 'Take care of him; and whatever more you spend, I will repay you when I come back. Which of these three, do you think, proved neighbor to the man who fell among the robbers?" He said, "The one who showed mercy on him." And Jesus said to him, "Go and do likewise." (Luke 10:25-37)

IN OUR FIRST section we reflected on the meaning and cost

of following Jesus. Our reflections were guided by the various questions of Jesus: the meaning of human existence, the identity of Jesus, the cost of following Jesus, keeping fellowship with the suffering Jesus, and loving Jesus in our daily lives. In this section we shift the focus but not the meaning of following Jesus. We want to reflect on what it means to love our neighbor. The New Testament is clear on this point: it is in loving our neighbor that we love God. The first letter of John says it so beautifully: "The man who does not love is among the living dead. Anyone who hates his brother is a murderer, and you know that eternal life abides in no murderer's heart" (1 Jn 3:14-15). There can be no separation between love of God and love of neighbor. Loving God and neighbor are intimately connected. Again the first letter of John: "If anyone says, 'My love is fixed on God,' yet hates his brother, he is a liar. One who has no love for the brother he has seen cannot have love for the God he has not seen. The commandment we have from him is this: whoever loves God must also love his brother" (1 Jn 4:20-21). Jesuit theologian Karl Rahner puts it this way:

> There is no love for God that is not, in itself, already a love for neighbor; and love for God only comes to its own identity through its fulfillment in a love for neighbor. Only one who loves his or her neighbor can know who God actually is. And only one who ultimately loves God can manage unconditionally to abandon himself or herself to another person, and not make that person the means of his or her own self-assertion. (*The Love of Jesus and the Love of Neighbor*)

The noted social philosopher Ashley Montagu once remarked in a public lecture, "Today there is so little love behind all the talk of love." Professor Montagu made a telling point. The word love has become threadbare today. The word love is overextended and misapplied. The preacher and the congregation often grow weary with its mention. For the preacher it has all been said before. For the congregation it has all been heard before. In our everyday lives we realize how much the word love is abused by those who seek to manipulate and control others. Love is often confused with lust. Much of our love-talk remains just talk and theory. Love-talk that never achieves love-action becomes that well known "noisy gong, a clanging cymbal." Yet love is the essence of God and the distinguishing characteristic of the Christian. We cannot give in to fatigue and cynicism which has grown on so many of our virtues. We must persist in talking about and doing love. The issue is not between love and something else. We *must* love. The issue is to try and see more clearly (though we always do so imperfectly) what is meant by love.

In trying to gain some insight into love, we must be honest and state that love is a *mystery* which always transcends our poor attempts to define it. Often the best we can do is to describe love in a general way and then live love in the concrete particulars of our lives. Love is the calling of every human being. Love is what we do when we are most completely ourselves — human beings made in the image and likeness of God. While love is the vocation of all human beings, love is that which radically individualizes me as a unique gift of God. No one is called to love like me in my particular circumstances. Love never remains an idea. Love becomes incarnate in a living, unique human being. In that way, love is my calling to be most authentically myself. Through love I become who I am and I fulfil a dream God has for my life. By loving, I help to make God's will in heaven part of the reality of life on earth. Love is never merely human but is also theological; that is, love involves us with God. The first letter of John tells us that "God is love." Each of us is made in the image of the God who is love and called to grow into the likeness of that love.

Love is the calling of every human being. We humans are also free beings; in fact, without freedom love could not be our vocation and we would not be human. God does not create robots. God creates human beings who are called to love God and neighbor in real freedom. Because we enjoy real freedom, we can refuse our calling to love. We can refuse to respond in love to the God who first loved us. We can limit and restrict our love to a select few. We can risk love (which is neither risking nor loving) only when it will be returned or acknowledged. We can show love only when it is in our interest. In all such instances we fail to dream God's dream for us — to love as He loves. It is in the willingness to love unconditionally that we draw close to God. Father Karl Rahner, S.J., writes: "Fundamentally all sin is only the refusal to entrust oneself to this measurelessness; it is the lesser love which, because it refuses to become greater, is no longer love." Sin, in other words, is the refusal to expand and grow. Such stretching involves pain and the letting go of past certainties. Love challenges us to move into an unknown land and find our neighbor in the face of those we once regarded as strangers and even enemies.

The beloved parable of the good Samaritan, recorded by St. Luke, powerfully describes our vocation to love all people as brothers and sisters. This parable highlights a distinguishing concern of Luke: the transvaluation of values and a reversal of what is normally expected to occur. Luke tells us of a God who is full of surprises and will not be controlled by human expectations and values. Jesus comes to fulfill the words of Isaiah the Prophet:

> "The Spirit of the Lord is upon me,
> because he has anointed me to preach good news to the poor.
> He has sent me to proclaim release to the captives

and recovering of sight to the blind,
to set at liberty those who are oppressed,
to proclaim the acceptable year of the Lord." (Lk 4:18-19)

Jesus, by word and deed, indicates that the kingdom of God is bursting forth. The outcasts, sinners, the poor, and those who exist on the margins of society are being welcomed as part of God's people. Those whom the self-righteous and pietistic have rejected have found favor with the Lord. Jesus comes to say that Yahweh does not judge by human standards and will not conform to our agenda. The hour of the unexpected is tolling. One must decide. Either continue to live in such a way that we try to manipulate God to our demands, or let go and let God be God in our lives.

The questions of Jesus are anything but meaningless. They raise crucial issues about the quality and destiny of our life. Jesus never asks a question in order to trap people or make them look foolish. Jesus desires that we take seriously the gift of our existence. However, we see in the question of the lawyer to Jesus one that is academic and seeks to trap Jesus. Maybe Jesus will give a blasphemous answer. Maybe His own words can be used against Him and He will be discredited in the eyes of all. Yet Jesus will not engage in such idle chatter. He simply invites the questioner to answer his own question. The lawyer responds in the traditional way: the fulfillment of the law is the love of God with one's whole being and the love of neighbor as oneself. Jesus commends his answer and invites him to act accordingly.

However, St. Luke tells us the lawyer wished "to justify himself." The lawyer in our passage represents a mind-set which refuses to acknowledge human dependency. The lawyer stands for all who approach God with their achievements, successes, and worldly trophies on display. Self-righteousness is a spiritual disease which refuses to acknowledge the need for forgiveness and grace. The self-righteous are those who believe there is no salvation outside their own efforts. In effect, justification is not the work of God in Jesus but something to be achieved by effort, good works, or birth in a chosen people. Eternal life becomes something that God *owes* me. Heaven is something that I can claim in justice. Such a mind-set refuses to acknowledge God as the loving Father who gives good things to all who ask. Ultimately the Cross of Jesus is rendered powerless.

From the heart of self-righteousness proceeds the idle question by the lawyer: "And who is my neighbor?" Jesus refuses to engage once again in verbal sparring or an academic discussion of theology. Jesus tells a story. This story, or parable, is one that challenges the conventional wisdom and self-righteousness of those who "know" what God is about and what groups are morally acceptable. The self-righteous "know" that God only associates with the righteous and those worthy of His attention. Naturally, the groups that are so favored are the ones to which I belong. Very neat. Too neat. Jesus tells a story that subverts these certainties and invites us to look at reality in a different way. Jesus' story challenges us to rethink what the Really Real is up to in our world. Those who are expected to be heroes turn out to be goats. Those from whom we expect little surprise us with heroic acts of virtue. The moral and intellectual barriers we construct are the idols that God's grace smashes. God is not a respecter of human judgments. The God Jesus tells us to call Father is filled with surprises.

Unfortunately the parable of the Good Samaritan has become too familiar to us. We have heard it all before. The shock and challenge of the parable have lost much of their bite. Yet the problem does not lie with the story, but with us. The self-righteous lawyer "knew" who his neighbor was — the one worthy of his love. The neighbor was the fellow Jew, the lawyer, or a member of his immediate family. Above all, the neighbor could never be a Samaritan. The morally acceptable folk are fellow lawyers, law-abiding Jews, the Levite, and the priest. Samaritans need not apply. Jesus rejects this too neatly ordered world. The Levite and priest fail in the moral requirement of neighborliness — caring for one in need. It is the Samaritan who proved to be the neighbor. It is the Samaritan who was moved to pity. The Samaritan did not allow the barriers of culture, history, and religion to prevent him from showing love. He saw a fellow human being in need, a need he could meet.

The Samaritan brings the man who fell among robbers to an innkeeper and says: "Look after him, and if there is any further expense I will repay you on my way back." With these words we obtain a glimpse into the character of this Samaritan. He is a man of generosity and trust. He does not place a limit on his compassion. Whatever further expense is needed in order to restore the victim to health will be paid. The Samaritan reveals the generosity of God to us and the generosity God expects us to show one another. The gift of Jesus reveals the unbounded love of God for us.

This generous love is not something we earn because we are morally good or belong to the right group. God is generous in love because that is the divine nature. St. Paul writes to the Romans: "It is precisely in this that God proves his love for us: that while we were still sinners, Christ died for us" (Rom 5:8). And again in the same chapter: "For if while we were God's enemies we were reconciled to God by the death of his Son, much more, now that we are reconciled, shall we be saved by his life" (Rom 5:10). The reconciling, healing love of God has bound up our wounds and restored us to the condition of

God's children. All of this is done because God is love and God loves us!

The parable of the Good Samaritan ends with a commission by Jesus: "Then go and do the same." For the person who professes faith in Yahweh and Jesus, there is no alternative: we must be compassionate and loving toward our neighbor. The neighbor and love must be without restriction or planning. The barriers of hatred, religion, culture, sex, age, race, economic status, and all the other restrictions to love must be dissolved. The Samaritan has to overcome the past and risk love to the one in need. Years of training in fear and distrust were transcended by love. So it is with us.

Who are the neighbors in need in our own world? Who are those whom we are tempted to pass by or ignore? Who are those in need of healing, a word of acceptance, and the gift of reconciliation? Who are those who feel the judgments of others and are in desperate need of forgiveness? In all of these and countless other situations we meet our neighbor. And for Christians, we meet Jesus as well.

The world today is in need of our Christian witness to love each person as a brother or sister. The other person is not hell, someone to be manipulated, or an adversary to be conquered in the name of class, race, or creed. The other is a fellow human being who is loved by God, redeemed by Jesus, and filled with the Holy Spirit. We Christians do not have all the specific answers to the problems of war, violence, poverty, and oppression. What we do have is the gift of our own life and the vision of what God intends for His good creation. We do not come to the world filled with social programs and solutions for balancing the wrongs of history. We come to the world learning Christ and His love for all people. Is not such talk refusing to acknowledge the enormous injustice in the world? Not at all. The Christian unites with fellow believers and those of good will to continue the story of the Good Samaritan. We look at the world through the eyes of love. We labor in love to overcome the barriers erected by fear and years of hatred. We replace the egoism of self and social structure with the witness of love. Human beings do make a difference. The works of Dorothy Day and Mother Teresa give powerful witness to what one person can do when moved by the love of Christ.

Maybe none of us will receive the Nobel Prize or serve soup in New York's Hell's Kitchen. Yet our lives make a difference nonetheless. As we journey to office, church, school, club, and home, the neighbor continues to lie by the side of the road waiting for someone to respond. We can engage in legalisms or intellectual word games about who is our neighbor and what is required of us. Jesus cuts through all of this avoidance. The neighbor is *anyone* who needs us and for whom we can make a difference. Christian love is oblivious to merit or worthiness. Love draws us to those who need healing. The Samaritan knew this. Blest will we be if we go and do the same.

CHAPTER 7

'If you love those who love you, what credit is that to you?' (Lk 6:32)

"But I say to you that hear, Love your enemies, do good to those who hate you, bless those who curse you, pray for those who abuse you. To him who strikes you on the cheek, offer the other also; and from him who takes away your cloak do not withhold your coat as well. Give to every one who begs from you: and of him who takes away your goods do not ask them again. And as you wish that men would do to you, do so to them.

"If you love those who love you, what credit is that to you? For even sinners love those who love them. And if you do good to those who do good to you, what credit is that to you? For even sinners do the same. And if you lend to those from whom you hope to receive, what credit is that to you? Even sinners lend to sinners, to receive as much again. But love your enemies, and do good, and lend, expecting nothing in return; and your reward will be great, and you will be sons of the Most High; for he is kind to the ungrateful and the selfish." (Luke 6:27-35)

IF GOLD IS tested in the fire, then the ways we respond to the enemy are the fiery test of our Christian love. In our previous chapter we indicated that love is our calling as human beings made in the image and likeness of the God of love. We can nod our agreement as long as love is extended to the family member, fellow believer, friend, associate, or countryman. However, the parable of the Good Samaritan challenges us to stretch our love to the neigh-

bor as anyone who needs us and for whom we can make a
difference. Even on this point we can nod agreement. We
can reach out to the stranger, foreigner, and to those who
feel unaccepted. We may even send money and offer
prayers for those in faraway places with strange-sounding
names. Yet more is required. Love must be stretched to
the limits of human expectation, calculation, and reason.
Jesus challenges us to love the enemy; to do good to those
who hate us; to bless those who curse us; and to pray for
those who treat us badly.

To love one's enemy strikes us as downright unnatural
and, in an age of psychologism, unhealthy. It is hard
enough for us to love the members of our family, spouses,
friends, and neighbors we see daily. But to require that we
love the enemy; that we love the family member who
made off with our inheritance, the spouse who has grown
cold or even unfaithful, the so-called friend who has betrayed our trust, the neighbor whose dog litters our lawn,
seems too much to ask from our all-too-human condition.
There are limits. And this is certainly one. Besides, to love
one's enemy is not psychologically healthy. Loving one's
enemy involves us in a lot of denial, repression, and unhealthy covering up of emotions. It is much more honest to
be true to our feelings and fight fire with fire. It is better
to give ulcers than to get them. Hence, the enemy must
know my wrath.

What can Jesus and St. Luke be up to with challenges
to love our enemies? St. Luke first. Luke is writing his
Gospel after the Neronian persecutions (A.D. 64) some-
time around the year 75. The Christian communities of
Greece and Asia Minor are under attack by the Roman authorities. Christianity, however, is not a political move-
ment that challenges the power of Caesar. Rather, the
Christian community is one in which Jesus is proclaimed
as Lord. All men and women are called to be part of God's

family. The Christian is living in an unfriendly environment. Jesus is the norm for how one is to act. Christians remain faithful to the memory of Jesus by living lives of simplicity, poverty, compassion, forgiveness, and joy. Above all, the Christian is faithful to Jesus when he or she loves as Jesus loved — completely. Jesus loved the sinner and the saint; the publican and the Pharisee; and the disciple as well as those who go away because they are rich. Jesus is able to say from the cross: "Father, forgive them; they do not know what they are doing" (Luke 23:34). The memory of the Cross must continue in the historical community or church. As Jesus forgave those who nailed Him to the cross, so the Christian is to forgive those who continue to nail, scourge, and kill.

All of the above may help explain Luke, but what about Jesus? What is Jesus up to with such hard sayings? If we read carefully the Sermon on the Plain (in the Gospel of Matthew it is termed the Sermon on the Mount and is contained in chapters five through seven) we notice that Jesus does not offer the disciple the comfort or moral status of *victim*. Being a victim (a title much coveted by contemporary society) is not a title the Christian has time to cultivate. For all who follow Jesus, there are more important things to do than go to court or seek revenge. Those who are hated, cursed, maltreated, slapped, ripped off, and the one from whom too many beg are *not* victims. They are given the opportunity to overcome evil by that alone which is stronger — love.

The Christian cannot engage in self-pity or nurse the desire for revenge. Rather, the Christian has the responsibility to act in such a way that evil is transformed and not increased. Christians are to do this by loving the enemy: blessing those who curse us; forgiving them who maltreat us; turning the other cheek, giving to the beggar without hope of return; and in general, doing good daily to all whom we meet. It cannot be stressed enough: Jesus is placing the responsibility of proper action on the one whom our world calls victim. It is the Christian who must transform the world and not be conformed to the world.

Jesus brings our passage to a close with a most dramatic saying: "Love your enemies and do good, and lend expecting nothing in return; and your reward will be great, and you will be sons of the Most High; for he is kind to the ungrateful and the selfish." Jesus is indicating that the disciple is to continue the good news of God's forgiving love. This continuation is not to be done by words, loving those who love us, and lending with the hope of a return and more. Rather, it is by loving in the most irrational (by human standards) way that we live as God's children. God's love is not for the worthy, the achiever, the morally superior, or the member of the in-group. In fact, God's love is for the one who is most in *need* and often does not realize how much the divine love is needed. Jesus has table fellowship with all the wrong folk: sinners, pagans, women of ill repute (are there ever men of ill repute?), tax collectors, and poor fishermen. Of such as these is the Kingdom of God comprised. The Christian as a child of God is expected to have fellowship with the enemy, the forgetful borrower, the ungrateful, and the wicked. Why? Because God does so. Furthermore, how else will those on the margins of society and Church experience God's love if not by our own loving of them?

Yet the doubts persist, and the old rationalizations return: did Jesus really mean what He said? Maybe Luke (or Matthew) misquoted Jesus (again not an uncommon contemporary complaint)? Every translator is a traitor, and so maybe something was lost in the translation. For the more sophisticated, we can always claim that Jesus thought the end of the world was near and so for the short term this was required conduct. However, since the end didn't come as quickly as anticipated, all demands are off. Accommodation and compromise are required. These tough demands must be tenderized so we fragile humans can digest them. If St. Augustine could pray for chastity, but not yet, why can we not also love our enemy — but not yet? We will love the enemy tomorrow when we are stronger, more confident, and more spiritual. But as with justice, love delayed is love denied. The words of Jesus are not to be trivialized or compromised. The Christian is to turn the enemy into a friend by the power of love. To borrow the words of G.K. Chesterton: "Who, if not you? When, if not now?"

On the practical, everyday level of life, how do we go about loving the neighbor? The words and life of Jesus do not offer us a detailed prescription of how to act in each situation. Jesus offers a vision — a way of being-in-the-world-with-others — that challenges much of our contemporary philosophy and pop psychology.

Two of the most influential philosophers of the modern period are Friedrich Wilhelm Nietzsche (1844-1900) and Jean-Paul Sartre (1905-1980). For the German existentialist Nietzsche, authentic existence is achieved through the will-to-power. "God is dead," cries Neitzsche, and now we must become gods determining right and wrong and the meaning of existence. Others, and the world as a whole, must be dominated and brought into subjection under my will. Life is a conflict in which the strong-willed survive and become Supermen. With Nietzsche's philosophy, it is not love which is extended but pure will. Each person I encounter is one whom I will dominate or the other will dominate me. From such a perspective each person is the enemy of the other. Meekness is weakness. The slave morality of Christianity, with its emphasis on forgiveness and compassion, must be overcome by the master morality which urges power, domination, and the will to win. Anyone or anything that obstructs my will must be destroyed.

For Nietzsche, each person is an enemy to be controlled or one who will control me by his or her superior will. For the French existentialist Sartre, each person is a tormentor. In one of his most famous plays, *No Exit* (1944), Sartre popularized his views on love and social relationships. *No Exit* has only three characters, a man and two women, one of whom is a lesbian. They have all died and find themselves in a bright room with three sofas. They are in hell! There are no flames to consume them, rocks to make them repent, or even Dante's blocks of ice to isolate them. Quite the contrary. They are stuck together forever in this one room. They will torture one another by their presence. At the end of the play the male character says, "Hell is other people."

Why is the presence of the other hell? For two reasons! First, the other looks at me and forms judgments about me which limit my freedom. The look of the other, his look of judgment and analysis, restricts what I can become. Secondly, the other always remains a mystery to me; someone whom I can never completely know. There is in the deepest love and friendship always a barrier behind which I cannot venture. In the final analysis, all love is doomed to failure. Love is nothing more than possession and loss of freedom. Our human relationships end in one of three ways for those who "love": masochism (I am the slave of another); sadism (I am the master of another); or indifference (the other does not even rate a look). Sartre goes on to commend Marxism as the only hope of achieving authentic social relations. All else is bad faith and bourgeois hypocrisy.

The existential philosophies of Nietzsche and Sartre have influenced much of our pop psychology and "how to" approach to social relationships. In the spirit of Nietzsche,

we are told to look out for number one, pull our own
strings, and win through intimidation. In the spirit of
Sartre, we must be our own best friend, say no and not feel
guilty, and avoid commitments. Life is a series of isolated
episodes of short duration. To such worldly wisdom, the
question of Jesus can be paraphrased: "If you dominate,
manipulate, ignore, or possess the other as an object, what
credit is that to you? If you hate and bring hell to others,
what is so authentic about that?" Jesus came to bring life
in abundance. The abundant life is not to be found in the
powerful will, the Marxist religion, or the pulling of
strings. Jesus invites us down a path less traveled, and
that can make all the difference.

Jesus invites us to fellowship with Him in the will to
love. While others may sometimes be hell, others are also
heaven. The other we call the enemy is a special opportunity to keep fellowship with Jesus. Jesus came as the Father's Word, His love letter, to proclaim the Kingdom and
good news. The Prologue of John's Gospel tells us that
"his own did not accept him" (Jn 1:11). The world was not
receptive to good news. The calls for change and conversion were as unpopular then as they are now. Jesus'
mission was to call the lost ones to the Father's house. The
self-righteous and those who saw Jesus as a threat to their
power rejected him. The forces of darkness turned Jesus
into an enemy. Jesus' response was one of unbounded love
and unfailing hope that hearts of stone would become
hearts of flesh. Jesus continued to go about doing good and
waiting for the blind and deaf to see and hear with their
heart.

The Christian story is one which invites us to love as
Jesus loved. We must desire for the enemy to become a
friend. In the thirteenth chapter of John's Gospel, Jesus is
having a last meal with His disciple before He dies. Judas
is present. John tells us that Jesus knows Judas is about to

hand Him over. Yet Jesus does not banish Judas, reject him, or hand him over to the disciples for an equal measure of violence. None of these. Jesus offers Judas the first morsel from the dish. Jesus is offering Judas a final chance to turn from darkness to light, from hatred to love. Judas has been given the power to hand Jesus over, but he has no ultimate power over Jesus. That is, no amount of evil can stop Jesus from loving or from drinking the cup of the Father. And Judas remains free to go into the night and betray the One who is Light and Life. We cannot force others to extend or accept forgiveness. We cannot coerce the enemy to become our friend. However, we can refuse to return hatred, violence, and evil. In so doing we love as Jesus loved and continue His presence in our world.

By way of concluding these reflections, let me offer the following as some ordinary, everyday ways of relating to the enemy in the spirit of Jesus.

1. Try to see in the other what God sees and loves. Each person is made in God's image and likeness. No one is born as "a bad seed." We become less than what God dreams for our lives by the decisions we make and the ways in which we respond to the changing circumstances of life. However, God never gives up on us. God continues to send opportunities for us to change. The most powerful occasions of grace are the gifts of other human beings. Each of us has the opportunity to help the person who sees the world as a jungle to see it as part of God's good creation. By our words and deeds we help continue the miracle of love. Nowhere is this more dramatic then when enemies become friends and love drives out all fear.

2. The enemy becomes a friend when we open our hearts to the Spirit and risk love. Make no mistake about it, love is a risk. We are afraid, and with good reason, of rejection, misunderstanding, and the appearance of weakness. To love, and most especially to love the enemy, re-

quires that we risk being vunerable in the presence of the other. We say in effect, "I am refusing to let hate have the last word in our relationship. I want to move our identities from enemies to friends. Even in the face of reasonable fear, I am going to gamble that you are just as afraid as I am and you want to be friends just as much as I do." There are no guarantees with love. There are guarantees with hate and fear. We ultimately lose!

3. The Epistle of James shows prudent regard for the human tongue. He writes, "See how tiny the spark is that sets a huge forest ablaze! The tongue is such a flame" (Jas 3:5-6). Our words can cut deep and deeply divide. The slings and arrows of our wrath can be as deadly as the neutron bomb. Thoughts and words are the parents of our deeds. It is very difficult for us to love another, much less the other who is an enemy, if we are filled with feelings of anger, bitterness, and resentment. It is next to impossible to become friends with the enemy when our thoughts are for vengeance and getting even. Words of kindness and forgiveness move us a significant step closer to deeds of love. Let our words of hatred be transformed into words of prayer for ourselves and the enemy.

4. Finally, to love the enemy in the spirit of Jesus means that we must *actively* love the one who wrongs us. We cannot love in some abstract, Platonic way. Christian love is fleshly and concrete. Christian love is human and always on the lookout for opportunities to be of service. We cannot be content with good thoughts, words, and feelings. We must be always ready to respond with love-in-action to the needs of the enemy. Christian love is as real and specific as the enemy who needs me. Again to paraphrase G.K. Chesterton, the Christian story has not been tried and found wanting, but found hard and left untried.

Who is your enemy? That's just another way of asking who is your soon-to-be friend.

CHAPTER 8

'When they could not pay, he forgave them both. Which will love him more?' (Lk 7:42)

One of the Pharisees asked [Jesus] to eat with him, and he went into the Pharisee's house, and sat at table. And behold, a woman of the city, who was a sinner, when she learned that he was sitting at table in the Pharisee's house, brought an alabaster flask of ointment, and standing behind him at his feet, weeping, she began to wet his feet with her tears, and wiped them with the hair of her head, and kissed his feet, and anointed them with the ointment. Now when the Pharisee who had invited him saw it, he said to himself, "If this man were a prophet, he would have known who and what sort of woman this is who is touching him, for she is a sinner." And Jesus answering said to him, "Simon, I have something to say to you. And he answered, "What is it, Teacher?" "A certain creditor had two debtors; one owed five hundred denarii, and the other fifty. When they could not pay, he forgave them both. Now which of them will love him more?" Simon answered, "The one, I suppose, to whom he forgave more." And he said to him, "You have judged rightly." Then turning toward the woman he said to Simon, "Do you see this woman? I entered your house, you gave me no water for my feet, but she has wet my feet with her tears and wiped them with her hair. You gave me no kiss, but from the time I came in she has not ceased to kiss my feet. You did not anoint my head with oil, but she has anointed my feet with ointment. Therefore I tell you, her sins, which are many, are forgiven, for she loved much; but he who is forgiven little, loves little." And he said to

her, "Your sins are forgiven." Then those who were at
table with him began to say among themselves, "Who is
this, who even forgives sins?" and he said to the woman,
"Your faith has saved you; go in peace." (Luke 7:36-50)

DURING THE summer I teach a college seminar entitled,
"Jesus and the New Testament." Naturally, the topic of
love is not far behind or long left off the agenda. During
one session I asked the students what they considered the
most difficult aspect of Jesus' message. After some silence, looking at notes, and shifting looks, a young lady
spoke up: "I find most difficult the idea that God's love is
a forgiving love. How can God really forgive me or someone like Hitler? I know that Jesus and the Church say God
forgives and loves us. However, such an idea is hard for
me to accept."

My college friend made an observation not uncommon
to many of us. For all of us — from the priest in the confessional to those in the dwindling lines of confession — the
notion of a God who loves and forgives is hard indeed. But
perhaps harder still is what God's forgiving love requires
of *us*. To draw from the comments of another of my college students: "God's forgiving love is great. What concerns me is, Jesus expects me to love in the same way. I
must confess it takes great courage to really pray the
Lord's Prayer. I mean, we say, 'Forgive us our debts as
we forgive our debtors.' Many times I just found it hard to
forgive and forget."

The observations of my students can help us to understand the Phariseee Simon in our reading from St. Luke.
Their observations can help us to understand that part of
our spiritual world view which reflects Simon. Fundamentally, Simon has what in modern terminology would be
called "a God problem." The problem, of course, is not
with God but Simon's idea or story of God. And Simon's
story of God is the ground which guides his relationships

with others. Just what is Simon's story of God? And secondly, how does this story of God influence the way he treats Jesus and the penitent woman?

Simon's God is the God of human justice and expectations. Simon's God does not associate with sinners or people with bad reputations. Only the good and the virtuous have a right to God's presence. God is only for the strong and those who know the law. Hence, the God of Simon is one who demands absolute obedience to a given set of regulations in order to guarantee moral virtue. This is the story of a God who lays burdens on men's shoulders (and women too! An equal-burdening God, no doubt). The yoke is heavy. Conformity to these rules is expected. The test of fidelity is the degree to which one pleases the God of external obedience.

However, such an image of God must fall under the weight of its own illusion. In the final analysis the God of Simon can be respected, obeyed, and feared. Yet the God of Simon can never be loved. Love is too dangerous to be permitted. Love is unpredictable, generous, spontaneous, and more than a little indifferent as to one's moral worth. Love is creative and often extends beyond the limits of our all-too-rational calculations of justice. Love does not ask the question of merit but the question of need — who needs my love? The God of Simon has no room for love or forgiveness. Without falling victim to the perils of playing armchair psychologist, we can only wonder how much anger and hatred Simon feels for such a God. Simon is under enormous pressure to do the right thing and obey all the rules. Watching his every move is the God who will "get ya" if you fail to touch all the legal bases. In the final analysis, such a God is rejected as oppressive and dehumanizing. Worst of all, God becomes our enemy. Duty and obedience without freedom and love are incomplete.

The story of God we carry in our heads has a way of in-

fluencing the way we relate to our fellows. Simon is not all
that different from the God he worships. Simon, like his
God, is judgmental and self-righteous. Simon thinks to
himself, "If this man were a prophet, he would have
known who and what sort of woman this is who is touching
him, for she is a sinner." The whole of the woman's identity is associated with her being a sinner. Furthermore, we
notice that Simon is devoid of graciousness, hospitality,
and the signs of welcome that makes a guest feel at home.
There is no water, kiss, or oil. The invitation to dine with
Simon is dry, loveless, and lacking in the bonds of human
community. Simon relates to his guests the way his God
relates to him.

By contrast, the woman who is known as a sinner carries with her a different story of God. Her story of God is
one with the story Jesus comes to proclaim — the love of
God is non-judgmental and forgiving. In the story of the
penitent woman in Luke's Gospel, we find five (5) aspects
of love that can enrich our spiritual life:

1. All genuine love requires the *courage* to take risks.
We cannot help but admire the fortitude of this unknown
woman. No one disputes that she is a sinner. The local
gossip mill has labeled and libeled her. She has a soiled
identity, and no one who wishes to avoid contamination
will associate with her. The unwelcome sign is hung wher-
ever she goes. She is an outcast. However, none of this
matters to her. Jesus is near, and into His presence —
even in the house of a Pharisee — she must go. No doubt
heads turned, faces were distorted in disbelief, and the
murmuring of self-righteous indignation was anything but
discreet. In spite of all this social pressure, the woman
goes to Jesus in hope of being forgiven. She will not be deterred.

2. All genuine, forgiving love requires that we become
liberated from the past and open to the future in hope.

Again, this woman is a sinner. It would be easy for her to accept this as her fate. Once a sinner, always a sinner. She could decide to live in the past and be ruled by sin. The past is powerful. The force of guilt is one that keeps us from being open to new ways of living and relating to God and others. This woman is a person of few words. She is a woman of action. She brings in the perfumed oil; she weeps; her tears wash Jesus' feet, and she dries His feet with her hair. Once the power of the past is broken, we can respond to God's invitation to live a new way. Contrition is necessary, but not sufficient in itself. We must live in the newness of God's love.

3. The love of this woman for Jesus mirrors the *generous* love of God for us. This woman is extravagant in her ministering to Jesus. She brings in an expensive vase of perfumed oil and anoints Jesus' feet. Her tears are so great that they can be used to wash the feet of Jesus. By human standards, this is too much. Our rationalistic self wants to caution moderation and prudence. Such extravagance causes us to become suspicious and look for a hidden agenda. However, this woman understands better than most how God loves us. God loves us in just such an extravagant, generous, and unbounded way. God gives Himself to us totally in the person of Jesus. The love of God and the contrition of this woman will not fit into our neat categories of how sinners and God should act.

4. God's love brings *peace* to the troubled heart. The fruit of reconciliation is the gift of peace. Peace is not the absence of conflict or tension. Peace is God's gift to those who labor to heal broken hearts and relationships. Such healing and the subsequent gift of peace are only possible for those who truly forgive from the heart. It is never enough to "let bygones be bygones," or to forget the past only on January 1st. Forgiveness is a daily need. True forgiveness means that we acknowledge the past hurts and

allow them to be healed. We cannot just bury the past; we must accept it and move beyond it. This is what Jesus is telling the woman: "Go in peace and live in a new way. Your past is real, but it need not imprison you forever. God's forgiving love has liberated you and healed you. Salvation has found its way in your heart. Now you shall experience true peace."

5. Finally — and what is most crucial to our reflection — forgiving, non-judgmental love allows one to risk *conversion*. Simon is incapable of acknowledging his sinfulness. He must play the role of moral policeman and hold the sins of others before them. In Simon's so doing, his God may be too busy with others to notice *his* sins. Simon cannot risk conversion or change because his God is a God of perfectionism. There is no room for love in Simon's story of God; hence there can be no forgiveness and repentance. His God simply would not understand. The penitent woman's story is different. She can risk repentence, conversion, and the acknowledgment of her sins because she knows (experiences) God as forgiving love. God does understand human weakness. God is big enough to deal with our sins and offer us salvation and peace. The question is whether we are wise enough to accept our unconditional acceptance of God's forgiving love.

The penitent woman's story of God is not easy to accept. Simon's story finds more followers. Why? Because Simon's God can be controlled and manipulated. All we need to do is follow the game plan and conform to the rules and God will be neutralized. We can keep God at a distance. God need not invade our hearts and make demands on our everyday lives. God is confined to church and those areas of our life we label "religious." However, outside of church and those areas marked religious, God has no power of presence. He can be ignored. Simon's God may be tough to handle in the beginning, but in time Simon's God is easily domesticated and forgotten.

The God proclaimed by Jesus and experienced by the penitent woman refuses our compliments, bribes, or attempts to control Him. The God of Jesus is one who challenges our conventional wisdom and morality. The labels of sinner and saint, wise and foolish, good and bad do not seem to fit in clear and neat ways. This God does not desire our animal sacrifices, money, buildings, or even our fawning prayers. What the God of Jesus wants is much more radical — God wants us. God finds His way into our hearts and will not let go. God cannot be forgotten or restricted to certain times and places. God is the Lord of history, creation, and our hearts. All is His, and we wait in patient hope for that time beyond time when God will be all in all.

I would like to return to the comments of my two college students. My first student expressed trouble with the idea of a God who forgives and accepts us unconditionally. My second student sensed the implications of what it means to live one's life in relationship with the God of forgiving love. What can we say to them? These questions are not unrelated. Part of what troubles us about the God who forgives is the realization that we must be a people who forgive. We can only be such a loving and forgiving community to the extent that God's love and forgiveness cease to be an idea and become an experienced reality in our lives. We cannot love and forgive others if we do not experience God's love and forgiveness. If Jesus remains just an idea or someone whom we talk about but never talk to, then our ability to live and forgive is restricted. Jesus not only came to tell us about God's forgiving love, but He came to show us how God loves and forgives. Jesus comes for the sick and those who are in need of healing. Table fellowship, the forgiveness of sins, the driving out of evil spirits, and proclaiming God's reign to the poor are visible signs of God's forgiving, accepting love.

Perhaps the most difficult obstacle to overcome, in accepting God's forgiving love and forgiving others in love, is the willingness to accept ourselves as forgiven. The Psalmist cries out, "My sin is before me always: 'Against you only have I sinned. . .' " (Ps 51[50]:6). These words capture much of our experience. We are aware of our sins, our broken promises, infidelities, and firm amendments that seem to be cast in Jell-O. Even with the best of intentions, we know the weakness of the will. How do we respond to sinfulness of our condition? Three ways are possible.

First, in imitation of Simon, we can *deny* our sinfulness. We can shift the blame to others in hopes that God will not be concerned about our "little sins." We cannot acknowledge our limitations and sinfulness because this would be an admission that we are not perfect. And if we are not perfect, then we are not deserving of God's love. We deny our sinfulness because we believe that God's love is only for the perfect. Hence we must be on a constant search for those who have bad reputations and are known sinners.

Second, we can acknowledge our sinfulness as a way of *despair*. We have tried to love God and neighbor, but we seem to fall into the same old patterns and habits. There is no use in trying to foster a better relationship with God and others. The pull of the past is too strong, and guilt weighs too heavy on our hearts. A mood of fatalism sets in, and we deny our freedom to choose a different way. If sin is too strong, then we shall eat, drink, and be merry, for tomorrow we may die. Despair and fatalism lead to hedonism and living for the moment. Since sin cannot be overcome, then we shall squeeze as much pleasure out of life as we can.

There is a third way that stands in opposition to both denial and despair. It is the way of *deliverance*. The Psalmist just quoted goes on to say, "A clean heart create for me, O God, and a steadfast spirit renew within me. . . . Give me back the joy of your salvation, and a willing spirit sustain in me" (Ps 51[50]:12,14). The penitent woman in Luke's Gospel experiences such a deliverance. She does not deny her sinfulness. She is not deterred by the opinions of others. She will not let the past determine her present and future. Above all, this woman is one who loves, and because she loves she is capable of accepting and extending forgiveness. This woman, who was known in the town as a sinner, is now known in a new way — she is a woman of great love. She is a woman who accepts herself as forgiven and is able to love and forgive.

So it is with us. Jesus is the one who comes to deliver us from our real enemies — sin and death. This deliverance does not come at a cheap price. It will demand an ultimate love: a love that passes through death to new life. In the midst of guilt, sin, and the claims of death, Jesus says to us, "You are forgiven. You are forgiven, not because of your merits or good works. You are forgiven, not because you can claim such a healing in justice. You are forgiven because you are in *need* of forgiveness and acceptance. Because you have been forgiven by the One who alone makes forgiveness possible, you can lovingly forgive and accept yourself and others. Peace and salvation have come to your heart."

Can we hear these words of grace? Can we accept them? Can we share them?

CHAPTER 9

'For which is the greater, one who sits at table, or one who serves?' (Lk 22:27)

> A dispute also arose among them, which of them was to be regarded as the greatest. And he said to them, "The kings of the Gentiles exercise lordship over them; and those in authority over them are called benefactors. But not so with you; rather let the greatest among you become as the youngest, and the leader as one who serves. For which is the greater, one who sits at table, or one who serves?
>
> "You are those who have continued with me in my trials; as my Father appointed, so do I appoint for you that you may eat and drink at my table in my kingdom, and sit on thrones, judging the twelve tribes of Israel." (Luke 22:24-39)

IN THIS chapter, and the one that follows, we shall examine the centrality of *service* as a way of following Christ and loving one another. In chapter ten we will discuss the importance of service within the faith community. Of special concern will be the need for humble service in imitation of Christ by those who hold positions of leadership. This chapter will concern itself with service as it is carried out in the world of work. Unfortunately most of us do not think of our daily work as a form of service. Our work seems connected with a paycheck and the ability to buy what we want and need. Work is secular and outside the concerns of our relationship with God. Work is the world where the strong and crafty survive and the meek only inherit the dirt. Our everyday work world seems so devoid of God and the sacred. Yet we hope to examine this important aspect of our life-work and see in our daily labors a valuable source of spiritual nourishment. The world of work cannot be isolated from Christ and the Gospel. In fact, if our everyday world would seem so devoid of God, then it is most urgent for us to uncover God's hidden presence. And we must share that presence with others.

The question of Jesus — Who, in fact, is the greater? — has troubled the Christian and the community from the beginning. Concerns over success, symbols of status and power, authority, and the places of honor did not come with the dawning of giant corporations. From the opening pages of Scripture, humankind has never been satisfied to be human. Our history, often tragic, is one of our grasping to be more. Adam and Eve must be like the gods, knowing good and evil. However, they are not gods but humans. From the tower of Babel in the Old Testament to the new biology of the anxious world, we humans continue to grasp for that power that belongs to God. Our insecurity and lack of trust set our hearts after the power of this world rather than the providence of God. Jesus tells us that true greatness is not possessed by those who possess a great deal. True greatness is not to be found in the expected manner: reclining at table, kingly thrones, executive boardrooms, or the great halls of political power; rather, true greatness is found in humble service. Success and happiness come to those who follow the example of Jesus and serve others. Jesus challenges the law of struggling ascent with His example of loving descent into our human condition. Jesus freely gives up the symbols of kingly power and assumes our human condition. In the words of St. Paul to the Philippians, ". . .he emptied himself and took the form of a slave, being born in the likeness of men" (Phil 2:8).

Jesus shows us that true greatness comes to the one who uses his or her gifts not to make a dollar but to make a contribution.

Throughout the history of humankind, work has received much attention. It is not enough that we humans work; we must find *meaning* in our work. And here is one of the major problems facing the modern worker, the Church and society. What is the meaning of human work? What is the real value of what we do each day? How do we measure success? What does the Judeo-Christian tradition have to say about our daily work as a means of service? Simply put: What is the spirituality of our work, so that our labor can be true service to others and give glory to God?

Some have read the Bible and concluded that work is a punishment for sin. The book of Genesis is oft quoted: "Cursed is the ground because of you; in toil you shall eat of it all the days of your life; thorns and thistles it shall bring forth to you; and you shall eat the plants of the field. In the sweat of your face you shall eat bread till you return to the ground, for out of it you are taken; you are dust, and to dust you shall return" (Gen 3:17-19). The curse of work is mentioned in the same context as the penalty of death. Work is proof of paradise lost.

Some have read the Bible and fashioned it to the American experience. For almost two hundred years America was guided by and benefited from the so-called Puritan Work Ethic. Work was an essential means to avoid temptation and the idleness of the devil's workshop. Work coupled with the values of thrift, sacrifice, discipline, and sobriety naturally yielded a great deal of wealth. How was one to reconcile wealth with the Gospel? Easy: wealth became a sign of finding favor with God. The rich prospered because they deserved to prosper and received God's blessings as the divine seal of approval. The poor deserved to be poor because God was displeased with them. While there is much to commend in the work ethic and its values, carried to an extreme it became perverted. Our work became equated with personal worth. The more we worked and prospered, the more God was pleased with us. The poor were not just poor; they were considered lazy and sinful.

Two other views of work have received much attention: first, the countercultural view of work was prevalent in the '60s in America; and secondly, the Marxist view of work and the worker in the modern world has attracted many followers.

During the decade of the '60s (the so-called "Second American Revolution") the American way of life was called into question. Traditional values and institutions were found wanting by certain vocal segments of the population. Work was one such area of transformation and repudiation. Members of the so-called counterculture rejected work as middle-class and bourgeois. Work simply perpetuated an evil society which must be destroyed. Work was what the "Establishment" held important; hence it must be rejected. Above all, work was seen as a dehumanizing means of consuming goods and services. All of this would change with the "Greening of America" and the rise of "Consciousness III." In subsequent years the counterculture has been absorbed into the main culture. Many of the most vocal dissenters have become part of the Establishment. The long hair, flowers, and jeans have been transformed into three-piece suits and the drive to get ahead with an M.B.A. from a good business school.

Finally, work has occupied a special place in the economics of Marxism. Work in the modern setting, that is, the factory and large urban centers, has become dehumanizing. The modern worker is alienated from the various products his labor produces. Because of specialization, there is a loss of a sense of wholeness or satisfaction in producing something from start to finish. The modern understanding of work, with its emphasis on standardization, robs the worker of a sense of individuality. The fragmented workplace leaves the worker fragmented and alienated. His fellow workers are competitors seeking the rewards of a capitalist society. The owners of the means of production are out to maximize profit at the expense of the workers. All the worker has is his labor, which he sells to the highest bidder for a price. In the final analysis, the modern worker is left with a joyless soul.

These images of work-punishment for sin — a divine sign of moral goodness or moral rejection; a useless activity for the Establishment, and the cause of modern alienation — are not very encouraging. However, there is another way for us to experience our work and exist among our fellows. This other view of work is to see our daily laboring as a means of service, the understanding of work as service for others. In imitation of Christ, we are called to be among our brothers and sisters as those who serve. The Old Testament's word on work is much richer than the isolated passage from Genesis quoted above (work as the punishment for sin). The Old Testament understands Yahweh as one who labors or works. This working of Yahweh is especially evident in the story of creation and liberation. God is love, and the love of God extends into the creation of the world. God's love is the motive for creation and the sharing of His life with human beings. God is not a mass producer but a skilled, loving artist who fashions the world and us as a supreme act of love. In the words of Jesuit theologian René Latourelle, "Like every work of God, creation too is a nuptial act; that is, it is a gesture of love on the part of God who initiates a regime of covenant and reciprocity, and the gesture becomes increasingly generous because creation is but the first moment in the inclusive chronicle of salvation, the first salvific act that is prolonged through the incarnation and redemption until it culminates in the creation of the new heavens, a new earth, a new world.''

The God who creates is also the God who labors on behalf of liberation. The Old-Testament experience of Exodus indicated to the Israelites that Yahweh cares for His people. Yahweh will not sit passively by and turn His back on the cry of the oppressed. Yahweh's love and caring are *active* and call the people from bondage to freedom. The stories of creation and liberation reach their zenith in the person of Jesus. The Word becomes flesh in order to send forth the Spirit of the new creation and a rebirth through faith. Jesus makes visible the workings of creation and liberation. Jesus calls all men and women to be born anew in God's love. Through faith in Jesus as the Son of God, we have the hope of shared glory with Jesus *now* and in the future. But there is more. Jesus liberates us from the wilderness of sin and death. The New Exodus is effected by Jesus' death on the cross. The Israelites knew that Yahweh was powerful and that He cared for them. At the Cross we experience the depth of God's loving power and care. At the Cross we experience the ultimate work of re-creation and liberation. It is in the shadow of the Cross that we pass from death to life.

The work of the new creation and liberation is not frozen in time but must be extended through history until the Lord comes again in glory. Simply put: our daily laboring must be one with the work of Yahweh — Jesus. In our work we are called to continue the work of rebirth and the message of salvation. Our world of work is never merely the collecting of a check, the ability to buy things, a shelter against the future, a means for retirement, or even a sign that God is pleased with us. Work is our sharing in the divine works of creation, recreation, and salvation. Work is the process of humanizing and divinizing the good creation in preparation for the coming of the new creation. In the most profound sense, our work is sacramental; that is, it reveals the creative and saving presence of God. Again Father Latourelle puts it so well: "It is impossible to advance Ahead without turning to the Above."

At this point a strong objection can be raised: it is fine to talk about sharing in God's work of creation and salvation as the meaning of human work. Yet does such a meaning apply only to those who are engaged in explicit church work? Isn't this meaning of daily labor really for priests and nuns but not for the person who labors in the office, shop, university, hospital, or scientific laboratory? Do you really mean to say that the housewife, the sanitation worker, and the cop on the beat are called to share in the work of God? As much as this may run counter to our modern understanding of work, the answer is a resounding YES. And, what is more — it is precisely those who labor in the unspectacular and are often taken for granted who have a special opportunity to share in God's work. It is most especially those who seldom if ever recline at table who can closely imitate the One who lived among us as one who serves.

Examples of such quiet service abound, although they often go unnoticed. The mother who daily tries to make a house a home; the father who daily labors in order to provide for his family; the young person who devotes himself to studies in the hopes of making a contribution to society; the scientist whose research is done in solitude, away from the eye of the camera; the office worker who tries daily to bring Christ and joy to the routines of the day — these and countless other instances speak of a quiet heroism of service to others. In an age that courts the highly visible and yearns for the "Lifestyles of the Rich and Famous," such examples seem boring and empty. Yet, in reality, here is where the Lord is to be found. Jesus lives among us as one who serves. Few of us will have the opportunity to do great things as the world understands greatness. Few of us will appear on television talk shows or have statues carved in our honor. Yet each of us has the opportunity to do good things each day. In the many ways we can reach out to others, share burdens, and lighten the weariness of daily living, we do good for others. This often goes unnoticed. What is important, however, is that our names are written in the book of life.

We must also be aware that many people are able to serve others through their sufferings and crosses. Let me share with you the story of Miss Emma Phillips. Each Friday I have the opportunity to bring Holy Communion to Miss Emma, as she likes to be called. Miss Emma has been confined to her bed in a small apartment for the past six years. Miss Emma is seventy-one years old. One day I asked her how she was able to always be so joyful, and didn't she ever get down on life or God? Her answer was most eloquent: "Father Maestri, I have bad days and at times I get the blues, but I have never been down a day. You see, I have too much to do. God has given me a work to do." "But Miss Emma," I interrupted, "what is your work?" She looked at me with a smile of patience and said, "Just because I can't walk or get out of this room doesn't mean God has forgotten about me. My work is to pray for those who can walk and run." Her smile of patience turned to one of playfulness: "I have even been known to pray for priests; most especially those who bring me Communion." The life and example of Miss Emma reminds us all that faith, heroism, and love are still present in our world. In a time of cynicism and disbelief, such lives are "rumors of angels" and "signals of transcendence." Like Jesus, Miss Emma is in our midst as one who serves, and we are all the richer for her life.

To conclude, we love our neighbor not merely on Sunday and not merely in church. We love the neighbor where we experience our brothers and sisters in need. A very significant context for serving and loving others in the world of work. We Christians believe that work is more than a paycheck or a means to the so-called good life. Work is a way of following Christ by being in the world as one who serves. Our work need not be highly visible or recognized as important by the standards of the world. What is important is that we see God in all things and do all things with love.

In our next chapter we will continue the theme of service, but the context will be different. We will reflect on service within the Christian community. Such reflections are crucial for the faith-life of the community and for those who are entrusted with leadership positions. In many important ways, love began within the community. It is in the faith community that we are nurtured in knowing Jesus. By drawing strength from the community, we can go forth to love and serve the Lord and others. It is to service within the faith community that we now turn our thoughts.

CHAPTER 10

'Do you know what I have done to you?'

(Jn 13:12)

Now before the feast of the Passover, when Jesus knew that his hour had come to depart out of this world to the Father, having loved his own who were in the world, he loved them to the end. And during supper when the devil had already put it into the heart of Judas Iscariot, Simon's son, to betray him, Jesus, knowing that the Father had given all things into his hands, and that he had come from God and was going to God, rose from supper, laid aside his garments, and girded himself with a towel. Then he poured water into a basin, and began to wash the disciples' feet, and to wipe them with the towel with which he was girded. He came to Simon Peter; and Peter said to him, "Lord, do you wash my feet?" Jesus answered him, "What I am doing you do not know now, but afterward you will understand." Peter said to him, "You shall never wash my feet." Jesus answered him, "If I do not wash you, you have no part in me." Simon Peter said to him, "Lord, not my feet only but also my hands and my head!" Jesus said to him, "He who has bathed does not need to wash, except for his feet, but he is clean all over; and you are clean, but not all of you." For he knew who was to betray him; that was why he said, "You are not all clean."

When he had washed their feet, and taken his garments, and resumed his place, he said to them, "Do you know what I have done to you? You call me Teacher and Lord; and you are right, for so I am. If I then, your Lord and Teacher, have washed your feet, you also ought to wash one another's feet. For I have given you an example, that you also

should do as I have done to you. Truly, Truly, I say to you, a
servant is not greater than his master; nor is he who is sent
greater than he who sent him. If you know these things,
blessed are you if you do them." (John 13:1-17)

LEWIS CARROLL'S *Alice in Wonderland* has delighted and
challenged readers since its appearance, when a little girl
fell down the hole of a rabbit. There have been countless
interpretations of Carroll's story, but one thing seems
clear: the above-ground logic of Alice will not work in the
below-ground world of the rabbit. The concepts of time,
logic, language, mathematics, and space do not compute
in Wonderland. Alice finds that her well-ordered world has
been turned upside down and the order from above the
rabbit's hole has been turned into chaos below. Furthermore, the entire "Chain of Being" becomes inverted in
that inanimated objects talk and animals such as the rabbit give orders to human beings such as Alice. Things are
not what they seem. Alice cannot wait to find a key that
will unlock the door to a beautiful garden she can only see
through a keyhole. However, when she finally enters the
garden with the Queen of Hearts, she finds that things are
ugly and artificial. The seemingly beautiful red roses are
red because they are painted red. With all of these goings
on, it is easy to understand why Alice found the happenings
in Wonderland "curiouser and curiouser."

Simon Peter and the eleven who gathered with Jesus
for that Last Supper must have felt like Alice. Things were
getting curiouser and curiouser. Roles were being re-
versed; titles did not mean quite the same thing as they
once did, and values were undergoing a transformation.
Jesus gathers for a final meal with those whom He loves
and those who have followed Him for the past three years.
The disciples have eaten with Jesus on countless occasions.

Yet this time is different. There is a deeper sense of

fellowship, love, and finality. This meal is not going to be eating as usual.

John tells us that during the meal Jesus washes His disciples' feet. Jesus performs one of the most menial and lowly tasks. How can this be? This is Jesus, the one who first invited them to "come and see." This is the Jesus who turned water into wine, cured the sick, calmed the elements of nature, multiplied the loaves, tested the Pharisees in every confrontation, and raised Lazarus from the dead. This is the Jesus who we have come to know and believe is the Messiah. Jesus is their Teacher and Lord who is now performing a task of humble service and telling them they must do the same for one another. No doubt we blend our voices with that of Simon Peter: "Lord, are you going to wash my feet? . . . Lord, you are never going to wash my feet. I cannot allow you to do this. Hurry up and get up before the others get the idea you are weak. Suppose one of the Pharisees would come uninvited. He would probably think you had lost all sense of reality and how the Messiah should act. Forget about washing my feet." What Simon Peter says makes great sense to those who operate by worldly logic. However, Jesus is challenging those who wish to be in fellowship with Him to live a new way — the way of humble, sacrificial love. "If I do not wash you, you will have no part in my heritage."

After this strange action, Jesus asks us one of those troubling questions of His, "Do you understand what I just did for you?" Of course not. There is no earthly reason why Jesus should do such a thing. Yet are these reasons that transcend earthly logic? What can Jesus be up to by such a dramatic action? By way of trying to understand what Jesus has done for us, let us remember the reading from St. Luke in our last chapter. A dispute at the Last Supper breaks out among the disciples as to who is the greatest. Who is the one most loved by Jesus? Who will take over when Jesus meets His fate in Jerusalem? Who will make the decisions and control the purse strings? Jesus tells the disciples that the greatest is the one who serves. The most important one is the one who follows Jesus in humble service. True greatness is not to be found in the earthly citadels of power but in the often quiet, unnoticed ways of love.

We all know that talk is cheap. Action is required. The lesson must be taught by the One who is the ultimate Teacher. The lesson of ultimate love and discipleship cannot be misunderstood. Jesus presents to the disciples what biblical scholar Bruce Vawter, C.M., terms "a parable in action." The well-ordered world of role and status is turned upside down. The last are first and the sinners go into heaven before the self-righteous. At the Lord's table, those who are great are not found reclining in purple and royal splendor. The Host, Teacher, and Lord is to be found on the floor with a towel and basin of water. Jesus is among them as a servant. Jesus is the humble servant who washes the disciples' feet. Words are inadequate. Three years of intensive schooling in love are not enough. A crash course in back-to-basics is required. Jesus has to rise from the meal and *show* them what it means to do the will of the Father. True greatness means you are expert at washing feet!

We would like to think that sin and opposition to Jesus belong to the world. Within the community, all is well as Jesus is proclaimed Lord. However, as St. Luke, church history, and daily experience teach, there is a good deal of the world in the Church. The community of faith is not immune to the sins of disbelief, lovelessness, and indifference. Yet on this night of the Last Supper the final meal of love before Jesus is to die, Satan is present. Satan is present not only in the heart of Judas Iscariot. Satan is doing his best to destroy the heart of community life —

loving, humble service. Jesus washes the disciples' feet as a dramatic way of indicating how destructive *ambition* can be in the Christian community.

It is no accident that both Saints Luke and John include the story of Peter's denial and Judas' betrayal with Jesus' words concerning the need for humble service. For both Luke and John knew that there was more than one way to betray and deny Jesus. Jesus came as God's Word of unbounded love. Jesus stripped Himself of glory and became one like us. However, the mission of Jesus to do the Father's will — love — would have to continue after Jesus returned to the Father. This is the mission of the faith-community: to love one another and all who are in need of an imitation of Jesus. The community of disciples is to remain in the world to continue the ongoing revelation of God's love. Ambition and the grasping for earthly power and glory run counter to the story. If members of the community seek places of honor, titles of power, signs of recognition; argue about who is the greatest, and recline so as to demand service, then the abiding presence of Jesus is obscured. The community becomes a counter-signal to the way of Jesus and His call to humble service.

No doubt the objection will be raised: what is wrong with ambition? What is so bad about getting ahead and using one's talents? Is it not much worse to be lazy and not take the intiative? Didn't Jesus warn against burying one's talents? We in America are especially partial to ambition and good old Yankee ingenuity. America is America because of ambition, the creative use of talents, and the refusal to be overcome by circumstance. There is much to be said for all of this. Our generous, loving God has given us gifts in abundance. We certainly are to use our talents. Much of the quality of life we enjoy in America is the result of hard work and ambition. However, there is always a danger of losing perspective. The temptation is great to equate our personal worth and that of others with material possessions and titles of honor. Our judgment can become faulty, and we begin to discriminate unjustly against one another. This is not new. The Epistle of James had to confront a community whose vision became blurred by equating moral goodness with money. James writes:

> My brethren, show no partiality as you hold the faith of our Lord Jesus Christ, the Lord of glory. For if a man with gold rings and in fine clothing comes into your assembly, and a poor man in shabby clothing also comes in, and you pay attention to the one who wears the fine clothing and say, "Have a seat here, please," while you say to the poor man, "Stand there," or, "Sit at my feet," have you not made distinctions among yourselves and become judges with evil thoughts? (Jas 2:1-4)

James goes on to remind the community that God chooses the lowly and makes them strong. Worldly fame and power are not the standards by which God judges and selects those to do His will. The ultimate norm for community relationships is love in imitation of Jesus.

The Apostle Paul knew a great deal about community life and the things that weaken and strengthen that life. In reading the letters of Paul, we find not idealized pictures of Christian communities but the realism of human beings struggling to love the Lord and one another. In many of these communities we witness various doctrinal controversies about such things as the resurrection, marriage, dietary laws, sexual ethics, and how to deal with converts. However, throughout many of these letters, we also witness conflicts between members of the community. Factionalism, rivalries, and one-upmanship were all too common. The underlying cause for weakening the bonds of the faith community is ambition. The ultimate spiritual force that perfects community life is love. The Christian community at Corinth will serve as an excellent example.

St. Paul founded the Christian community at Corinth around A.D. 50. The Holy Spirit had blessed this community with many spiritual gifts. In the twelfth chapter of First Corinthians Paul lists these gifts: wisdom, knowledge, faith, healing, miraculous powers, prophecy, discernment, the gift of tongues, and the ability to interpret tongues. Unfortunately, gifts have a way of becoming possessions, and those who receive the gifts think theirs are special and superior to all others. Soon divisions arise and the community begins to break apart. Such divisions and rivalries adversely affect the celebration of the Eucharist. The sacrament of our unity and love becomes a sham. We cannot receive the Lord's love worthily while despising our brothers and sisters. We cannot eat at the Lord's table as His family if we are grasping for the symbols of worldly power and respectibility. The Eucharist is the revelation of Jesus' faithful love for us and the food that nourishes us for loving and serving one another. Regardless of our gifts, we come to the table because we are in need and dependent on the One who gives generously.

The Corinthian community is aware of its gifts but has lost sight of the One who gave them, and gifts remain gifts only as long as they are shared. Hence St. Paul, the good pastor, does not condemn the community or read them the riot act; rather, Paul wants them to remember that "To each is given the manifestation of the Spirit for the common good" (1 Cor 12:8). There are many gifts, but what is more important is the *unity* in love. There are many different forms of ministry, but everything is to be done in the name of the Lord. When ambition raises its ugly head, the results are disastrous. Paul wants it clearly understood that *every* gift and ministry is important for the community. Paul uses the analogy of the body. Each member has a specific function which is important for the health of the whole person. No one organ can do all of the functions of the entire body. So it is with community life. Together, and only together in the Spirit, do our individual gifts blend in order to insure spiritual well-being.

In one of the most profound and oft-quoted passages of St. Paul, chapter thirteen of First Corinthians, we are told that love is the greatest of gifts. All the other gifts of the Spirit only make sense when they are grounded in love. Apart from love, gifts become possessions and weapons by which we separate ourselves from one another. What is of the utmost importance from the perspective of Paul is this: while no one receives all gifts and all ministries, *all* are called to love. Love is the universal gift and the greatest of gifts. Love alone lasts. If one has many talents, and is able to bring many to Christ, but does not have love, one's life becomes "a noisy gong, a clanging cymbal." Without love, we come to believe it is *our* words, work, and ministry that are so effective. Without love, we come to believe that we are indispensible and we easily begin to preach ourselves. Only love keeps us from such folly. Only love keeps the One who is Love at the center of community life, gifts, and ministry. Only love overcomes worldly ambition and moves us to wash one another's feet and live in community as those who serve.

Divine ambition is a constant threat for the Christian community. History indicates that Jesus' example has often been forgotten or not understood. It is especially important for the post-Vatican II Church to keep the example of Jesus ever before us. A beautiful model of Church emerged from the Second Vatican Council — *all* the people of God make up the Church. Each baptized person receives a ministry, a charism, and the vocation to proclaim the good news of Jesus in his/her own situation. With this new appreciation of gifts and ministries, the importance of love cannot be overestimated. For Christian love prevents the destructive presence of ambition from taking hold. Love moves us to see how our gifts blend with those of others for the common good. Love allows us to share our gifts with others and to be open to the gifts of others. Above all, love allows us to *suffer* with our gifts. Yes, suffer. Father Karl Rahner, S.J., captures the mystery of gifts and suffering:

> A charism always involves suffering. For it is painful to fulfill the task set by the charism, the gift received, and at the same time within the one body to endure the opposition of another's activity which may in certain circumstances be equally justified. One's own gift is always limited and humbled by another's gift. Sometimes it must wait until it can develop, until its *kairos*, its hour, has come and that of another has passed or is fading. This painful fact is to be viewed soberly as an inevitable consequence of there being one Church and many gifts. *(The Spirit of the Church)*

The situation and makeup of the Church today are certainly more complex than 2,000 years ago. However, some things remain constant. The Spirit continues to give gifts for the common good. The acceptance of one's gift and ministry involves suffering. There is always the reality and danger of ambition and division. The need to wash one another's feet in imitation of Jesus is both timeless and timely. Leadership is still one of service in fellowship with the One who lived among us as Servant. Love is the greatest of gifts and one we are all given and meant to share. Even in an age of electronic churches, the question of Jesus is asked with power: "Do you understand what I just did for you?" Wise are those who really understand, and blest are those who put that wisdom into practice.

PART III

Fundamental Things Apply

CHAPTER 11

'Do you take offense at this?' (Jn 6:61)

"Truly, truly I say to you, unless you eat the flesh of the Son of Man and drink his blood, you have no life in you; he who eats my flesh and drinks my blood has eternal life, and I will raise him up at the last day. For my flesh is food indeed, and my blood is drink indeed. He who eats my flesh and drinks my blood abides in me, and I in him. As the living Father sent me, and I live because of the Father so he who eats me will live because of me. This is the bread which came down from heaven, not such as the fathers ate and died; he who eats this bread will live for ever." This [Jesus] said in the synagogue as he taught at Capernaum.

Many of his disciples, when they heard it, said, "This is a hard saying; who can listen to it?" But Jesus, knowing in himself that his disciples murmured at it, said to them, "Do you take offense at this? . . ."

After this many of his disciples drew back and no longer went about with him. Jesus said to the twelve, "Will you also go away?" Simon Peter answered him, "Lord, to whom shall we go? You have the words of eternal life; and we have believed, and have come to know, that you are the Holy One of God." (John 6:53-61; 66-69)

THE CENTRAL concern of our reflections is the questions of Jesus. These questions are not asked for idle speculation or pure academic exercise. The questions of Jesus touch on the deepest concerns of the human heart. Our first section centered on the meaning of human existence and how the meaning of our lives can only be known in light of Jesus Christ. Our second section indicated that the following of Jesus is always more than a vertical relationship or a comfortable spiritualism that excuses us from responsibility to *this* world. On the contrary, the following of Jesus means that we seek the hidden presence of Jesus in our brothers and sisters. Most especially, we find Jesus in the least of our brethren — the poor, hungry, naked, sick, imprisoned, homeless, powerless, and all who exist on the margins of our smug world.

In this our final section, we turn our attention to the fundamentals and go back to the basics of what it means to be human and to follow Jesus. All along we have contended that our vocation is to love and our destiny is to be one with the God who is love. Love is not abstract and confined by definitions or the categories of morality, which say who is to be loved and who is to be rejected. Christian love is known in practice, and it is practiced by every Christian toward all who are in need of love. The standard of Christian love is need, not merit. And the model of that love is Jesus, who cured the sick and had table fellowship with the outcasts. He did all of this not because they deserved to be healed or because they deserved His presence. Rather, Jesus drew near to all people simply because they *needed* Him and His love.

A word about fundamentalism and going back to the basics seems in order. Unfortunately many of our most prized words have been contaminated by misuse and abuse. For example, the word "discrimination." In recent times this word has come to be associated with prejudice and the unjust exclusion of certain individuals and groups on the basis of race, creed, color, sex, or national origin. "Discrimination" has come to acquire an almost totally pejorative meaning. However, discrimination can also mean that one possess a good sense of judgment or discernment. One is able to discriminate because one has a keen sense of what is of true value. The same unfortunate soiled identity has come to be applied to the word "fundamentalism" or the phrase "back to basics."

Usually when we hear the word "fundamentalism," the images and associated feelings automatically rush to the mind and brain. We have come to associate fundamentalism with reactionary religion and politics; the electronic church and the video vicars of television; anti-intellectualism, and Bible-thumping preachers who are seldom right but never uncertain. Its next of kin, "back to basics," is often taken to be a code expression used by those who hope to return America to some golden age. Those who propose such programs are often associated with being out of date or anti-modern and obstructing the progress so dear to our way of life. Hence, our visceral reaction to "fundamentalism" and "the basics" is one of revulsion.

Again, this is unfortunate. For the word "fundamental" has about it the notion of that which is solid and can be depended upon. Fundamentals are the essentials without which one cannot proceed in any work or course of study. Any sports watcher will tell you that the great teams are those who are sound in the fundamentals of the game: hitting, running, shooting, blocking, passing, etc. Any teacher will tell you that it's hard to read Shakespeare and do physics if one is not schooled in the fundamentals of literature and mathematics. Sometimes we tend to forget that no matter how majestic a building may be, it is only as good as the basement (foundation) on which it rests. When things go wrong in sports, the classroom, or the majestic building, it's good to review the fundamentals and get back to the basics. This is anything but reactionary. It is simply the prudence to return to the essentials so that one can proceed with success.

Naturally, there are those who give fundamental*ism* and the basics a bad name. Yet this ought not turn us off to the importance of those elements upon which the structures of our living, learning, and loving are based. With the above few paragraphs in mind, we want to turn our attention to the basics and fundamentals of the Christian life. Each of these aspects is grounded in love — the love of Jesus and the love of our neighbor. We want to examine the Eucharist, healing, and forgiveness. In addition, since the Christian story is incarnational, we want to reflect on the lives of two great disclosure models — Mary and John the Baptist. These two great followers of Jesus offer us much wisdom for our daily journey with the Lord. Let us turn our attention to the Eucharist and its meaning for discipleship.

The selection from Scripture which introduced this chapter comes from the sixth chapter of John's Gospel. The Fourth Gospel does not contain an institution account of the Eucharist. In place of such an account, John presents a reflection in the form of a discourse by Jesus on the Eucharist. Chapter six contains one of the longest of Jesus' discourses and concerns itself with the *meaning* of the Eucharist. This long reflection is usually referred to as the "Bread-of-Life Discourse." The entire discourse runs from 6:25 to 6:59. Also contained in chapter six are the multiplication of the loaves and Jesus walking on the Sea of Galilee at Tiberias.

Chapter six opens with John's account of the multiplication of loaves. Jesus takes a couple of dried fish and five barley loaves, gives thanks, and then distributes them to the five thousand. Not only are the five thousand fed, but there are twelve baskets left over (the abundant generosity of God is evidenced by this sign). However, Jesus must flee the crowds, for they wish to make Him king. Jesus is not a political Messiah or one who comes to provide *only* material needs. Jesus' primary mission is to reveal the name of the Father as suffering, faithful love. Later on in the day, the disciples of Jesus head for Capernaum by boat, crossing the Sea of Galilee at Tiberias. A storm comes up, and the disciples are frightened.

Jesus appears and calms the sea and their fears. The disciples, along with the crowd, finally catch up with Jesus in Capernaum.

The multiplication of the loaves provides Jesus with the opportunity to discourse on the *meaning* of this sign. The crowds have misunderstood Jesus to be a political savior or someone who is able to provide their material needs. Jesus, however, wants them to understand what has happened on the deeper level of the spirit. We are not saying that Jesus is unconcerned about the physical needs of the people. We are not saying Jesus is indifferent to political realities. From the perspective of John, all that is secondary. What is primary to the mission of Jesus is to reveal God's unbounded love for all people. The crowds have followed Jesus because they have had their fill of the loaves. Jesus invites this crowd to look for the food that never perishes and is the source of eternal life. Jesus is the New Moses who comes to give the people an eternal Manna, the food that will nourish them forever. Jesus had offered the Samaritan women the "living waters" of the Spirit, after which she would never thirst again (4:14). In this episode, Jesus offers the crowd the food of eternal life (6:27).

What is the deeper meaning of the multiplication of the loaves? How are we to understand this sign? What does it mean to receive the bread of eternal life? In order to answer these r these s, we will need to reflect on three aspects of the discourse: the meaning of the symbol bread, the sacrificial theme of the Eucharist, and the es-

chatological hope offered to all to eat Jesus' body and
drink His blood.

The symbol of bread has been associated in the Old
Testament with the wisdom of God. The association of
bread with the wisdom of God is very important in the
first part of Jesus' discourse (verses 35-50). The bread
that Jesus comes to bring is His revelation and teaching
about the Father. The bread that Jesus brings far sur-
passes that of the Old Testament. Jesus is the Word made
flesh. Jesus and the Father are one. Jesus is the Son of
God who has been entrusted with the mission of bringing
all people to know (experience) God as Love. Jesus has
told His disciples in chapter four, "Doing the will of him
who sent me and bringing his work to completion is my
food" (Jn 4:34). The completion of that work will be done
on the cross when the full revelation of Jesus as the Son of
God and the Father's name as suffering love takes place.

The symbol of bread takes on a new meaning in verses
51-58. The theme of the Eucharist becomes prominent in
these verses. Jesus is the living bread that is sent by the
Father to give eternal life to all who believe and eat at the
Lord's table. Jesus shocks the audience with His words:
"He who feeds on my flesh and drinks my blood has
eternal life and I will raise him up on the last day" (Jn
6:54). The flesh and blood of Jesus in the Eucharist are
like no food ever eaten. To eat the bread of this world is to
be satisfied only for a time. However, to eat the flesh and
drink the blood of Jesus is to be satisfied for eternity.
Whenever the Christian community gathers to celebrate
the Eucharist, it shares the real *food* and drink of Jesus.

The gift of Jesus to the Christian community in the Eucharist brings to us the theme of sacrificial love. The Eucharist is the eternal memorial of the suffering, unbounded love of God on the cross. The Eucharist is the historical reminder of the depth of God's love for us. This

love does not come at a cheap price but requires the ultimate giving — Jesus on the cross. To eat the flesh and drink the blood of Jesus in the Eucharist is to be in fellowship with the death of Jesus. St. Paul writes to the Christians at Corinth: "Every time, then, you eat this bread and drink this cup you proclaim the death of the Lord until he comes!" (1 Cor 11:27).

"Until he comes!" highlights the third theme of Jesus' discourse on the Eucharist. The Eucharist is food for both time and eternity, today and forever. To eat and drink at the Lord's table in the Eucharist is not merely to be in fellowship with the Cross of Jesus. Death is not the final word, no matter how heroic that death may seem. There is the hope of glory and the expectation of resurrection. To eat the flesh and drink the blood of Jesus is to live in the patient hope of being raised on the last day. Ignatius of Antioch called the Eucharist the "medicine of immortality." At our celebration of the Eucharist, we proclaim the great mystery of faith: "Christ has died. Christ has risen. Christ will come again." Our reception of the Eucharist is our visible act of faith that He will come again and that we will share in His glory.

Jesus gives this instruction in the synagogue at Capernaum. We might expect this powerful discourse to receive a favorable hearing. Such is not the case. John tells us in stark realism of the reaction of the congregation: "After hearing his words, many of his disciples remarked, 'This sort of talk is hard to endure! How can anyone take it seriously?' " (Jn 6:60). John goes on to report that "many of his disciples broke away and would not remain in his company any longer" (Jn 6:66). The faith of many of his disciples was shaken. These disciples continued to judge by the standards of the flesh rather than the Spirit.

Jesus does not compromise His message. He does not

take back His gift of suffering love — His own body and blood in the Eucharist. The disciples are free to walk away. Jesus does not coerce anyone into following Him. One can only come to Jesus in freedom and remain with Him in the same freedom. What is more, Jesus does not remove the Twelve from making the decisions as well. They too must decide if the words of Jesus shake their faith. They must decide if they will break away and not remain in His company any longer. Jesus says to the Twelve, "Do you want to leave me too?" (Jn 6:67). The answer of Simon Peter remains normative for all Christians: "Lord, to whom shall we go? You have the words of eternal life. We have come to believe; we are convinced that you are God's holy one" (Jn 6:68-69).

The question of Jesus (Does it — does my teaching and gift — shake your faith?") is not merely for those in the synagogue at Capernaum. The question is for us as well. Let us be not too quick to answer "No" and too quick to condemn those who kept company with Jesus no longer. Perhaps they understood better than we just what is involved in Jesus' teaching and the offering of Himself. If we answer "No" to Jesus and remain a disciple, let us keep the following three points in mind:

1. Jesus comes to teach and reveal to all peoples that God is love and God loves each of us in an unbounded way. Love means involvement and caring. Jesus is the living reminder that Yahweh is not a God of distance and indifference. He is a strange God. He makes a covenant. He chases after His people and demands that they remain faithful to Him. God is an active partner in our history and discloses Himself to us. God wants us to respond in faith and love. The Eucharist is God's continual gift of Himself to us. It is a new and eternal covenant of love that keeps ever before us the suffering love of God. Each time we gather to hear the word and break the bread and share the

cup we recall the great love God has for us. Yahweh and Jesus are not going to leave us alone to do our own thing. Yahweh and Jesus care about us too much. Their love for us is too strong. Again and again they come to us and offer us the gift of new life in the Eucharist. No doubt some found this a hard saying. Many people want a more distant, uncaring God who will allow their privacy. Not Yahweh and Jesus. They won't rest until we open our hearts to love.

2. The gift of Jesus in the Eucharist means we must change. To receive the Eucharist worthily means that we must live each day in a new way — the way of following Jesus. Jesus tells the congregation that to eat His flesh and drink His blood is to *already* possess eternal life. Life with Jesus is not a future promise only but a *present* reality in our lives. When we receive the Eucharist we are sharing in the meal that prepares us now for that future banquet in the Kingdom. Hence, we must live today as followers of Jesus. We must love one another now, care for one another now, and remain in Jesus now.

3. This brings us to our third point: namely, that Jesus' gift of Himself in the Eucharist is an invitation to love as He loves. That is, Jesus' life was one of daily being broken and poured out for others. The Eucharist is both the invitation to do the same and the food that strengthens us for such a witness. The words of Father Karl Rahner, S.J., capture the relationship between our reception of the Eucharist and the need for our personal love and sacrifice:

> Whoever receives the sacrament of Jesus' heart without preparing his own heart has missed Jesus completely. Such a person has misunderstood the meaning of *opus operatum*, and has degraded the Eucharist and the sacraments to mere magic. The sacraments have not been given to us to take the place of our own personal effort, or to make our effort easier! We can only approach the sacrament of the heart of Jesus Christ with an open heart. We can only re-

ceive the grace of the Eucharist insofar as we personally
also realize the sacrifice contained in it. (*Spiritual Ex-
ercises*)

The bread-of-life discourse continues to trouble us. Jesus
is offering us His very self as the true source of eternal
life. Maybe we do not walk away like those disciples whose
faith was shaken and who found the words of Jesus too
hard. Maybe our trouble is a different one. Have we become too familiar with the Eucharist? Have we taken this
great gift of love from Jesus too much for granted? When
we hear the words at Communion, "The body of Christ," is
our "Amen" a real statement of faith or just the expected
response? Do we receive the Eucharist and then promptly
forget what we have been given and called to share?

These are not easy questions. But then following Jesus
has never been easy. The Eucharist is Jesus' gift of Himself, the constant reminder of His unbounded love, and our
hope of resurrected glory. Does this shake your faith? Let
us pray that we make the words of Simon Peter our own:
"Lord, to whom shall we go? You have the words of
eternal life. We have believed, and have come to know,
that you are the holy one of God."

CHAPTER 12

'What do you want me to do for you?'

(Lk 18:41)

> As he [Jesus] drew near to Jericho, a blind man was sitting by the roadside begging; and hearing a multitude going by, inquired what this meant. They told him, "Jesus of Nazareth is passing by." And he cried, "Jesus, Son of David, have mercy on me!" And those who were in front rebuked him, telling him to be silent; but he cried out all the more, "Son of David, have mercy on me!" And Jesus stopped, and commanded him to be brought to him; and when he came near, he asked him, "What do you want me to do for you?" He said, "Lord, let me receive my sight." And Jesus said to him, "Receive your sight; your faith has made you well." And immediately he received his sight and followed him, glorifying God; and all the people, when they saw it, gave praise to God. (Luke 18:35-43)

JESUS IS ON His last journey to Jerusalem, where the authorities are waiting to have their way with Him. Jesus must pass through Jericho. In so doing, He comes across a blind man begging. A noisy crowd is following Jesus, and the excitement is felt by the blind man. After being informed it is Jesus of Nazareth, the blind man boldly requests Jesus to take notice of him. The crowd tries to silence him, but the blind man will have none of it. The blind man becomes more vocal. Jesus inquires what the man wants Him to do. The man wants to see. Jesus pronounces the man's sight restored. All praise God, and even the former blind man follows Jesus. A nice story with a great ending. Granted things will get sticky in Jerusalem, but for now Jesus is having things His way. Is there something more to Luke's story than merely a calming episode before the storm? Let us reflect on this story and its relevance for the importance of healing within the Christian story.

The blind man is a character both interesting and inspiring. Three aspects of his story deserve our attention. The blind man is determined, courageous, and insightful.

First, the blind man is determined to catch Jesus' attention. His one great opportunity is near, and he will not allow it to pass him by. There are many obstacles to be overcome: he is blind, he is a beggar, and the crowd wants to silence him and spare Jesus this nuisance. The blind man has many problems, but none will stand in the way of his possible cure. The more the crowd tries to silence him, the more determined he comes. Voices are raised telling him to be quiet and wait for some other time and some other passer-by. The blind man perseveres and cries out, "Jesus, Son of David, have mercy on me!" It would have been easy to give in to self-pity and group pressure; but not this man. Here is his chance to start life anew, and no one will stop him.

Secondly, the blind man is courageous. Part of the conventional religious belief of the day held that suffering and infirmities were punishments for sin. No doubt many in the crowd believed that this man was not only a nuisance but a sinner. He has no rights. In the presence of Jesus, he must keep silent. The blind man will have none of it. Jesus asks what seems at first blush a meaningless question: "What do you want me to do for you?" Doesn't Jesus know the man is blind and wants to be healed? Whether Jesus knows what the man wants or not is not the issue. The blind man must petition Jesus for what he wants. This man has the courage to ask Jesus, not for money, but for that which will restore him to the demands of daily life. This request, "I want to see," can only be made by a man of courage.

What is so courageous about requesting his sight? Sight is such a precious gift we take it for granted. This man hopes to see his loved ones, the morning star, the setting of the sun, and the everyday world that until now has been veiled. Yet the request to see will also make this man subject to the demands and responsibilities of everyday life. He will not be able to beg. He will have to get a job and care for his own needs. This man will no longer be excused from the burdens of the sighted. Compassion will be withdrawn. In fact, some may come to resent this man's good fortune. Hostility will replace pity. We humans become comfortable with our problems and demons. We make friends with them. Change is so frightening because we must give up the familiar. All right, but one certainly would want to give up bad things. Yes, *if* we could be certain that the bad we are giving up is not going to be replaced with the worse of the unknown.

We can become comfortable with our infirmities. We can also use our disabilities to punish others. Let me tell you the story of Laura. Laura is a bright, attractive middle-aged housewife with two children and a loving husband. Laura has suffered with arthritis since she was in her thirties. Recently her physician indicated that she would need an operation on her badly deteriorating knee. The operation was somewhat standard, and recovery time would be two weeks in the hospital and four weeks of home therapy. After that time Laura should be in excellent condition. No doubt she would feel better than she felt before. Her husband, David, and the two children would do the necessary chores around the house while Laura was recovering. All in all, a rather routine situation.

The operation was performed with great success, at least from the standpoint of Doctor Davies. The deformed bone was removed, and Laura should be walking in six weeks or sooner. At least that was the plan. While in the hospital, Laura was cooperative and faithful to her therapy. However, something changed when she returned home for final recovery. Laura refused to do her therapy and was refusing even to see the therapist who came three times a week. Laura seemed content to lie in the bed and let her leg grow weak. All the while David and the children were busy with the housework and exhorting Laura to "get with the program" and "return to normal."

Finally, David was beginning to reach the breaking point. He had to work all day and then return home to Laura and the needs of the family and the daily demands of housekeeping. The children were becoming concerned as well about their parents' arguments, which were becoming more heated and of longer duration. It seemed when they were not fighting they were not speaking either. Something had to give. David came to the rectory and told me his story. He was hoping I would go and discuss the situation with Laura, since she and I were very good friends. I agreed that things were bad and getting worse. So off I went.

I visited Laura and found her unusually withdrawn and even bitter. No amount of probing or clerical cheerfullness seemed to help. She limited her answers to "yes" and "no." I had the feeling Laura wished I would vanish. Before I left, a crazy question popped into my head: "Ask Laura why she is trying to punish David and the children." I caught myself and turned that one over in my head several times. (Jesus could ask such questions, but I was not sure I was up to the task!) Finally I blurted it out: "Laura, you seem so angry with everyone. You have closed yourself off from family and friends. You have stopped your therapy. David and the children are tired and confused. I have the feeling you are trying to punish them or teach them some lesson they have not quite grasped. Are you trying to hurt them? What is going on with you anyway?''

I waited for the angry words and the command to leave I knew were coming. They never came. Laura remained silent. As I walked to the door, she said, ''You are right, you know. I want to teach David and the children a lesson. Maybe I have hurt them too much. Maybe. . . .'' Her voice trailed off, and she began to cry softly, as if she had come to learn some painful lesson.

I asked Laura why she was crying. She replied, ''This is the first time I have cried since the operation. For the past twenty years I have done everything I could to make David happy and help make the house a home for our children. I am just not sure it has been worth it.''

I interrupted. ''Laura, of course it has been worth it. You have a loving husband and two wonderful children. Many women would be happy to be in your situation.''

''Really?'' Laura replied in a question full of mock surprise. ''I just do not think David and the children appreciate what I do. I don't think they know who I am and what I need from time to time. I guess I am just being a selfish middle-aged female. But that's the way I feel.'' The crying stopped and Laura continued to stare straight ahead.

After a few minutes I asked Laura, ''Do David and the children have any idea how you feel?'' She replied, ''I don't think so. I've never really mentioned any of this before.'' For all these years Laura had been carrying her resentment about the felt lack of concern by David and the children. The resentment did not go away; it just waited for the right time to explode. The surgery was the perfect outlet. Now David and the children were learning a lesson, but at the time they still did not know what it was. Laura, of course, was learning a lesson as well.

I spent a few more minutes with Laura and then proceeded to have a chat with David. He was sincerely shocked by what I had to say. The children seemed less confused once I explained what their mother was going through. All of them agreed that they had taken Laura for granted. Her work was just expected and often went unappreciated. They could not remember the last time they'd told Laura how much they loved her and valued what she did for them. David and the children just presumed that Laura knew. Well, Laura did not. The situation had come to this point because of silence by Laura and presumption by David and the children.

What is one to do? For the first time in a long time Laura, David, and the children talked and listened to one another. It was painful. Old hurts and unspoken resentments had to be faced and healed. Emotional scars do not heal quite as quickly as those of the body. Yet an important first step was accomplished. Laura, David, and the children have a long way to go, but they are better off today then when David first came to see me. Laura wanted to teach David and the children a lesson. This she did; however, I know that Laura learned some valuable lessons as well. Silence can be golden, but at times it is fool's gold. David and the children learned how important it is to appreciate those who love us and humanize our daily lives. We all need to hear and say how important we are to one another.

To return to the blind man, the third characteristic of note is his insight. The ability to see is not a faculty limited to the eyes and physical reality. When the crowd grows in excitement about Jesus, the blind man wants to know what is going on. He is told that "Jesus of Nazareth is passing by." The blind man does *not* address Jesus in this manner. Rather, he cries out, "Jesus, Son of David, have mercy on me!" The blind man calls out to Jesus with the messanic title "Son of David." Although at present he cannot see Jesus as the crowd sees him, the blind man understands Jesus to be the Messiah. Jesus acknowledges that the blind man is a person of spiritual insight, and that his faith has healed him. Healing is more than merely the restoration of a physical or emotional handicap. Healing is spiritual and gives witness to the presence of God. The Kingdom of God is visibly present in Jesus, and the healing of those who are sick, infirm, or troubled is proof of that presence.

In our reflections about healing, we must say a brief word about sickness. Sickness and subsequent suffering can never be localized to a given organ or area of the body. Sickness affects the whole person — mind, body, and spirit. Sickness brings home to us how vulnerable we are, how limited in our powers to be the captain of our fate. Sickness seems so absurd and useless. Sickness and pain narrow our world and isolate us from others. Sickness invites the pain of loneliness. Sickness, especially of the innocent, raises the deepest of religious questions: "Why?" Sickness can bring about feelings of guilt: "My cancer is a punishment from God"; "I am ill because of my past sins." In other words, sickness is never merely a physical or psychological condition. It involves the whole person. The way we understand our sickness, the story of our sickness, offers a valuable insight into our character and spiritual strength.

If sickness involves the whole person, then so does healing. The coming of Jesus is the story of the healing power of love. The words "healing" and "salvation" are related. To heal is to save, and in being saved we are healed. St. John writes in chapter three of his Gospel: "For God so loved the world that he gave his only Son, that

whoever believes in him should not perish but have eternal
life'' (Jn 3:16). Jesus comes to tell us and show us how
much God cares for us. Jesus' message is not one of condemnation but one of forgiveness and healing. The healing
message of Jesus does not come at a cheap price. The
prophet Isaiah writes about the Suffering Servant: ''But
he was wounded for our transgressions, he was bruised for
our iniquities; upon him was the chastisement that made
us whole, and with his stripes we were healed'' (Is 53:5-6).
The passion and cross of Jesus serve as the ultimate testimony of Jesus' reconciling, healing love.

Even before the Cross, we see in the ministry of Jesus
His healing love at work. And this love heals the whole
person — mind, body, and spirit. Physical infirmities are
no less worthy of our concern than spiritual illness. Very
often a physical illness can be a threat to our spiritual
well-being. Jesus loves us in the entirety of our being. No
aspect of our lives is excluded from the healing presence
of Jesus. Jesus cures the blind man, relieves Peter's
mother-in-law of a fever, and heals the lame man on the
sabbath at the Sheep Gate pool (Jn 5:1ff). Jesus forgives
sins and has table-fellowship with the outcasts of society
and synagogue: the penitent woman (Lk 7:36-50); the
woman caught in adultery (Jn 8:1-11); Zacchaeus, the tax
collector (Lk 19:1-10); and the healing of the leper (Mt
8:1-4). Jesus cures those suffering from severe emotional
and spiritual disorders: the cure of a demoniac (Mk
1:23-28); the Canaanite woman's request for her small
daughter (Mk 7:24-30); and the exorcism of the possessed
boy (Mk 9:14-28). The effects of the healing ministry of
Jesus are recorded by St. Matthew: ''And great crowds
came to him, bringing with them the lame, the maimed,
the blind, the dumb, and many others, and they put them
at his feet and he healed them, so that the throng won-
dered, when they saw the dumb speaking, the maimed

whole, the lame walking, and the blind seeing, and they glorified the God of Israel (Mt 15:30-31).

The healing ministry of Jesus has been entrusted to the Church, and to each of us. St. James writes in his Epistle: "Is any among you sick? Let him call for the elders [presbyters] of the church, and let them pray over him, anointing him with oil in the name of the Lord; and the prayer of faith will save the sick man, and the Lord will raise him up" (Jas 5:14-15). In today's world of miracle drugs, high technology, and medical wonders, we often overlook the power of prayer in healing. Health is more than the absence of an illness or injury. It is a sense of well-being, of wholeness. To be healthy is to be an integrated human being. We cannot overlook the importance of prayer and the love and support of community. We cannot ignore the needs of the spirit. The human person is more than matter and that which can be quantified through various medical procedures. The wise physician models his ministry after that of the Divine Physician — healing the whole person.

Each of us through our baptism is called to continue the healing ministry of Jesus. How can this be? We do not have the power to raise the dead, expel evil spirits, restore sight to the blind, and forgive sins. Such a ministry is for a select few and seems only to have happened on rare occasions in former times. Yet each of us is called to be an instrument of God's saving, healing love. The rare occasions are really very commonplace. And the former times are now! How often each day do we pass time with those in need of our healing words and deeds? The young person who is blind and confused about a future choice; the young couple who are struggling to make their marriage a covenant of love; the elderly person who feels "out of it" and useless in a world dominated by the Pepsi generation; the sinner who needs to experience God's forgiveness; the depressed person who needs someone who understands; the terminally ill patient who needs to know she is still alive and life-giving; the leader who is struggling with loneliness and the burden of unpopular decision-making; the person of conscience who must take a stand on principle and not convenience; and the religious whose ministry has known many crosses — all of these and countless other examples are instances when we can be an instrument of healing. A word of encouragement, challenge, or acceptance can restore one to well-being. A smile, a touch, or just our physical presence can mean so much to those who are often forgotten in our up-and-doing world. Far from being rare, the opportunity for being a person of healing surrounds us each day.

Jesus asks the blind man, "What do you want me to do for you?" (Lk 8:41). The blind man has the persistence to ask for sight and the courage to accept his healing. The same question comes to us: "What do you want Jesus to do for you?" Like the blind man, we need to persist in the face of opposition and we need the courage to accept our healing so as to live a new life. Let us also pray that we can be instruments of God's healing love in our daily lives. "Jesus, let us be instruments of your healing love. Let us bring words and deeds of kindness to those in need. Let us supply sight to the blind, comfort to the broken-hearted, guidance to the confused, and strength to those who are weak. Let us bring your grace to those who need acceptance and a word of welcome. Help us to extend the sign of peace and the kiss of welcome to those who are alienated. All the while, let us know that your work is being done through us."

CHAPTER 13

'How is it that you sought me? Did you not know that I must be in my Father's house?' (Lk 2:49)

Now his [Jesus'] parents went to Jerusalem every year at the feast of the Passover. And when he was twelve years old, they went up according to the custom; and when the feast was ended, as they were returning, the boy Jesus stayed behind in Jerusalem. His parents did not know it, but supposing him to be in the company they went a day's journey, and they sought him among their kinsfolk and acquaintances; and when they did not find him, they returned to Jerusalem, seeking him. After three days they found him in the temple, sitting among the teachers, listening to them and asking them questions; and all who heard him were amazed at his understanding and his answers. And when they saw him they were astonished; and his mother said to him, "Son, why have you treated us so? Behold, your father and I have been looking for you anxiously." And he said to them, "How is it that you sought me? Did you not know that I must be in my Father's house?" And they did not understand the saying which he spoke to them. And he went down with them and came to Nazareth, and was obedient to them; and his mother kept all these things in her heart."

And Jesus increased in wisdom and in stature, and in favor with God and man. (Luke 2:41-52)

MARK TWAIN once greeted his audience with the following line: "The rumor of my death has been greatly exaggerated." The same could be said of the American family. Its obituary has been written by many. The conventional wisdom holds that the family is obsolete; the family no longer serves the needs of modern society or the modern individual (this is especially true of the individual, so the storyline goes, since the family is authorit*arian* and restricts one's freedom). Monogomous marriage, fidelity, and children have gone the way of Ozzie and Harriet. New realities and new rules (which are often no rules at all) seem to be the order of the day: "trial" marriage; responsible parenthood (translated, this usually means no children or only "wanted children," which is basically the same); working mothers with latchkey children; and the rise of single-parent dwellings. All of these occurrences and countless others announce the death of the American family as we know it. The extended, Walton-type family (with spouses, children, grandparents, and even cousins sharing the same roof) and more recent nuclear (spouses and children — usually two at most) family arrangements have made their contributions. However, this is a new day. We have come of age in the brave new world.

Yet, in the midst of such doom and gloom, something interesting is taking place: the importance of family, traditional marriage, sexual fidelity, and a more receptive attitude toward children has reappeared. There has even been a slight decline in the divorce rate and the number of abortions in America. Sociologists and social philosophers (a very important book is *The War for the Family* by Peter and Brigitte Berger) have written extensively on the tenacity of family life. And what is more, these sociologists are also moving from description to evaluation. They are saying that it is a *good* thing that family life and values associated with the family are making a comeback. To the purist of social science, this is anathema. Values should not enter into research (this itself is a value judgment). The sociologist should just report and let others form the policies. Values are messy and private. They are hard to quantify. However, one of the most important

American sociologists was C. Wright Mills. Mills wrote that sociologists must do more than report what is going on. They must enter the moral dialogue of our society. Mills was hoping to restore to sociology the moral tradition of the classical sociologists Emile Durkheim and Max Weber (a very interesting book on the importance of a moral vision in doing sociology is Richard Means's *The Ethical Imperative*). Durkheim and Weber were not satisfied to just report the facts. They felt a moral responsibility to evaluate the facts and make proposals for the future. Likewise, Mills, drawing on this classical tradition in sociology, was asking his colleagues to be imaginative and committed. Mills was challenging the social-scientific community to come from behind their charts and data. Many commentators and researchers on the American family are doing just that.

The Christian tradition has consistently understood the family as something more than a piece of sociological data or an economic unit of production. Sociological analysis of the family is crucial if the church is to meet and anticipate real family needs (the research of Father Andrew M. Greeley is a case in point). Yet while such analysis is necessary, it is not sufficient. The family has a mission, and a place within the unfolding of the Kingdom of God in history. The family is crucial for the moral, religious, and spiritual formation of church members and disciples of Jesus. We have understood the family to be a community called to holiness. The Christian family is called to be like the Holy Family, that is, a family united in the Triune love of Father, Son, and Spirit.

In the next few pages we want to reflect on the spiritual meaning of family life in light of Jesus, Mary, and Joseph.

We also want to examine the spiritual dimensions of the family through the document on family life by the Second Vatican Council. And finally, we will present the spirituality of family life by Pope John Paul II.

At first blush it may seem in Luke 2:49 that Jesus is being arrogant or downright disrespectful toward His concerned parents. Mary and Joseph are upset that Jesus has become separated from them. They find Jesus in the temple conversing with the teachers of the Law. Mary wants to know why Jesus is here and not with them. He responds, "How is that you sought me? Did you not know I must be in my Father's house?" St. Luke goes on to say that Mary and Joseph did not understand Jesus' answer. Perhaps we can understand Jesus' question in a different way. Specifically, what is the Father's work that the family is entrusted with? How does family life aid in building the Kingdom and preparing the way for the Lord's return in glory?

St. Luke goes on to write that Jesus returned with them and was obedient. Jesus grew in grace and wisdom. Mary, the loving Mother, treasured all these formative experiences in her heart. From this little episode we see one of the most important works of the family, namely, to increase "in wisdom and in stature, and in favor with God and man." The family is entrusted with the mission of extending God's love in the world. By the various ways in which husbands and wives love one another and care for their children, a powerful witness of God's love is given to the world. The parents who dare to discipline, without being overly protective, teach their children virtues that last for a lifetime. Parents are to continue the work of Mary and Joseph by being the first teachers of their children about God's love. They do this by the eloquent example of their lives. Loving parents provide their children with a powerful witness (a sacrament) of God's unbounded love. Let us reflect briefly on the example of Joseph, Mary, and Jesus.

The witness of the New Testament tells us the Joseph is a carpenter by trade. A simple occupation for a man of great integrity. Mary and Joseph are engaged and living in a relationship of espousal, which lasts about one year. Naturally, they are not to have sexual relations during this time. However, Mary becomes pregnant, and this confronts Joseph with a problem: does he divorce her and make her infidelity known, or does he simply keep quiet and pretend to be the child's father? Joseph does neither. It would be dishonest to claim fatherhood for the child, and Joseph does not want to hurt Mary and hold her up to public ridicule. An angel comes to Joseph in a dream and says that it is God's will that Mary is pregnant through the Holy Spirit. The child is to be named Jesus and save His people from sin (Mt 1:18-25). We need not argue about whether an angel really came or if this is just popular tradition. What is crucial is Joseph's response: he is a man of integrity and faith. To place Joseph in the modern lingo: Joseph is a man who is secure in his identity and does not feel the need to be macho or self-pitying. Joseph loves Mary, and his love remains strong even in the face of some unsettling circumstances. There are no accusations or plans to get even. Joseph is also a man of great faith. He trusts that God's will is for the best. Maybe he does not understand everything fully. But he trusts God enough and loves Mary enough to go forth. He is strong enough to take risks. In beautiful simplicity, Matthew writes, "When Joseph woke from sleep, he did as the angel of the Lord commanded him; he took his wife. . ." (Mt 1:24).

So much has been written about Mary. Throughout the Church's history she has been honored as the Mother of God and the model of Christian existence. Mary is extolled as the woman of faith and the woman for others. In our brief passage from St. Luke, we are presented with a picture of Mary that is so humanly attractive. St. Luke cherishes the humanity of Mary and invites us to do the same. St. Luke offers us a beautiful insight into her character: Mary keeps all the early experiences of Jesus in her heart. Mary, like any mother, treasures the formative years of Jesus. Like any mother, Mary is very concerned and upset about Jesus being lost on their return from Jerusalem. When Mary finds Jesus in the temple, she says what any mother would say to a child lost and now found, "Son, why have you treated us so? Behold, your father and I have been looking for you anxiously." Jesus' response about being in His Father's house doing His Father's work doesn't help much; St. Luke indicates that Mary and Joseph did not understand His response. Is there any parent who has not been confused at the response of a child?

On a deeper level, Mary's reaction of anger and sorrow is a foreshadowing of what is to come. Mary will have to let go of Jesus at some future date. Even now we see Jesus growing in awareness of His mission. Jesus is sent to do His Father's will. Not the will of Joseph the carpenter, but Jesus must do the will of His heavenly Father. This means that Jesus must announce the good news of forgiveness and the joy of being a child of God. Unfortunately the good news of Jesus is bad news to those who love the praise of men more than the glory of God. Many of the religious leaders turn against Jesus and plot to have Him killed. Jesus' ministry will cause many sorrows to pierce Mary's heart. In this brief episode, Mary is experiencing a foreshadowing of what is to come on a more profound level. Mary treasures the temple episode in her heart, as she will treasure all that Jesus does. Once again we see even the suffering aspects of life must be treasured as a part of growth. Love allows such a treasuring to take place.

Not only is the humanity of Mary prized by St. Luke, but also the humanity of Jesus comes shining through. St.

Luke presents a picture of Jesus as a very precocious child. Jesus remains in Jerusalem, unbeknown to His mother and father. He is not to be found among relatives and friends who went with them to Jerusalem. Jesus seems to be very independent. We might expect Jesus to be terrified and panic-stricken in the city alone. Quite the contrary. Jesus is in the temple listening to lectures and asking questions. The teachers are amazed at His intelligence. Anyone who has taught knows the delight and the unsettling feeling of teaching a gifted child. Even Mary and Joseph are astonished at the sight.

Yet St. Luke goes on to remind us that Jesus is still a young boy who has much to learn and is in need of maturity. Mary and Joseph must have done their job well. For St. Luke tells us that Jesus "increased in wisdom and stature, and favor with God and man." Jesus does so because He returns to Nazareth with Mary and Joseph. He remains with them in obedience. Even precocious children are in need of obedience and discipline. Maybe more so. Yet what St. Luke is offering us is a glimpse of Jesus' whole life — a life lived in obedience to His heavenly Father. Jesus is obedient because He is capable, even at such an early age, of great love. Only those who love and are mature are capable of obedience. Unfortunately, today we have come to associate obedience with a loss of freedom and the failure to be one's own person. In the name of authenticity and our rights, we are very suspicious of obedience and authority. Granted, authority can be abused and easily slide into authoritarian*ism*. However, the abuse of authority is no argument against its legitimate presence. Likewise, we can escape from freedom and responsibility in the name of obedience. This is not the obedience that characterized the life of Jesus. True obedience requires trust and faith in another. Jesus did the will of His Father perfectly because He loved the Father perfectly. Jesus was obedient to His parents, and He "increased in wisdom and stature and grace before God and men."

The family of Jesus, Mary, and Joseph is the Holy Family because individually and as a community they are totally centered in God and the doing of His will. Joseph is a man of integrity who does God's will even though he has no certain answers or guarantees about the future. Mary is the servant of the Lord and the woman who in fear and trembling says "Yes" to God, completely. Jesus is the obedient son of His earthly family and heavenly Father. We see in them what we are called to become. We see in the Holy Family a community of faith, love, and obedience. Their real human family life gives us encouragement as we strive each day to center our lives in God. The Second Vatican Council and the Apostolic Exhortation of John Paul II (*Familiaris Consortio*, or *The Community of the Family*, 1981) offer us a powerful spirituality of and for family life. Let us briefly examine each of these.

The Second Vatican Council brought about many changes. One of the most significant and beneficial concerned the role of the laity in the life of the Church. The Council Fathers formulated a vision of Church which was inclusive of *all* people. The people are the Church. Each baptized person has the burdens and joy of preaching and living the Gospel. The laity have a vital role in the life of the Church and in helping to build the Kingdom of God. The Council went only to offer a beautiful spirituality of married and family life.

The Pastoral Constitution on The Church in The Modern World (Gaudium et Spes) speaks eloquently about the nobility of marriage and family life in the modern world (*Gaudium et Spes*, 47-52). The Council takes note of the serious obstacles to the proper fostering of marital and family life: abandonment of traditional values concerning sexuality and family; self-love and narcissism; hedonism; modern economic considerations; the policies of certain civil societies; and some areas suffering from population growth that has outrun resources. All of these factors and many others have caused concern among many in the Church. Yet the sacredness of marriage and the dignity of family life have endured. The Church has a mission and responsibility to preserve this sacredness and dignity.

The covenant of marriage is the gift of God. The union of husband and wife mirrors the love of Christ for His Church. Husband and wife are called to live a love like Christ: faithful, enduring, suffering, and Paschal. Husbands and wives are to die to their own desires and feelings and seek the needs of the other. Through such a dying the couples come to experience the joy of the resurrection and new life. The love of husband and wife is also fruitful; that is, the conjugal love of spouses yields new life. A child is both a result and gift of mutual life. Children are entrusted to parents and are to be schooled in the love of God, Church, and responsible citizenship. Through the proper educating of children, parents fulfill their stewardship of love and trust. Such educating extends beyond the so-called secular subjects and includes as fundamental the lessons of a living faith which help the child to grow in discipleship.

The document goes on to call the family "a kind of school of deeper humanity." The views of the roles of the mother and father are traditional. The father is to take an active role in the formation of the child. Yet the mother plays a crucial role in the religious formation of the child. The domestic role of the mother is highly valued. The document does not deny the legitimate role of women in other areas of society; rather, it *values* the domestic role of the woman as mother. The document goes on to praise the legitimate advances made by women in modern society. Both parents are responsible for the discernment and development of a vocation, especially to the religious and priestly life. The family is the foundation of society, and society has moral and civic duties to promote its well-being.

Finally, the document on the family has a special word for children and the respect they owe their parents. Children contribute to the wholeness of parents by the ways in which they acknowledge the benefits and sacrifices given by good parents. Such gratitude encourages parents and inspires them to greater acts of love and trust. Children must be ever mindful of the enormous love they owe their parents. Children must stand by their parents in time of suffering, hardships, and most especially old age. As parents have stood by their children in their moments of trial, so much children be faithful to their parents in their moments of need. The document on Christian family life contains the following worthy of meditation:

> Thus the Christian family which springs from marriage as a reflection of the loving covenant uniting Christ with the Church, and as a participation in that covenant, will manifest to all men the Savior's living presence in the world, and the genuine nature of the Church. This the family will do by the mutual love of the spouses, by their generous fruitfulness, their solidarity and faithfulness, and by the loving way in which all members of the family work together. ("The Sanctity of Marriage and the Family," *Gaudium et Spes*, n. 48)

Pope John Paul II has offered us a powerful spirituality and vision for Christian family life. In his Apostolic Exhortation, the Pope is keenly aware of the importance of the family to the well-being of society and Church. The bright spots and shadows of modern family life are highlighted. Marriage and family life are grounded in the love of God. Because the family is grounded in the Divine Love, there are fundamental tasks entrusted to the family. A brief word is about each is in order.

First of all, the family is a living community of persons. The power and goal of family life is love. If there is not love present, then there is no community and the development of persons is severely retarded. The fundamental need of all humans is to be loved and to give love. Pope John Paul II wrote in his encyclical *Redemptor Hominis*:

> Man cannot live without love. He remains a being that is incomprehensible for himself; his life is senseless if love is not revealed to him, if he does not encounter love, if he does not experience it and make it his own, if he does not participate in it.

Husbands and wives are to love and respect one another in mutual reverence. Their love is a sacramental presence of the faithful, fruitful love of Christ for the Church. John Paul goes on to this section to especially mention the dignity of women and the elderly in the family. Women are deserving of complete respect, their dignity honored. Unfortunately, society has done much to turn women into objects of exploitation and sexual abuse. The injustices of discrimination and the violence of pornography must be overcome. Finally, the elderly must never be treated as outcasts or useless burdens. The pastoral activity of the Church and the laws of civil society must do all in their power to honor those who have much to give. In honoring the elderly, we shall enjoy a long life in the land the Lord has given us.

Second, the family as a community of love is called to serve life. In so doing, the family participates in the work of the loving Creator. The conjugal love between husband and wife brings forth the gift of new life in the begetting of children. The giving of husband and wife to each other in marital love makes way for the miracle of God's presence and a new life. A child is a visible sign, a sacrament, of human and divine love coming together. The Christian family is the natural setting in which the child is introduced to Jesus Christ as the One who comes to bring life in abundance.

Third, the family is called to play an active role in the moral development of civil society. The family is "the first and vital call of society." The family has a moral responsibility to work for a more just and generous social order. The family should work for laws, institutions, and candidates that respect human rights, serve life, and respect the dignity of all persons. The family must be protected by society, and its rights vigorously protected.

Finally, the Christian family is called to share in the life and mission of the Church. The Second Vatican Council termed the family "the little church." Through the love and devotion of parents, the children come to know Christ and experience His healing love. The family is called to preach and live the Gospel daily. By such a life commitment, the Christian family becomes a believing and evangelizing community. Family life is an eloquent statement of the good news of the Divine Love.

We have come a long way in our discussion on marriage and family life. The life and example of the Holy Family may seem so distant and far removed from our modern experience. Yet in truth, the Holy Family has much to say to each Christian family. For holiness and love are the eternal goals of every family. These goals are only reached by centering oneself totally in God. The family is anything but obsolete. The family is the vital cell of society and the Church in miniature. The prayer of Pope John Paul II must be our own:

> May Christ the Lord, the universal king, the king of families, be present in every Christian home as He was at Cana,

bestowing light, joy, serenity and strength. On the solemn day dedicated to His kingship, I beg of Him that every family may generously make its own contribution to the coming of His kingdom in the world — "a kingdom of truth and life, a kingdom of holiness and grace, a kingdom of justice, love and peace," toward which history is journeying. (Given in Rome, at St. Peter's Nov. 22, 1981, the solemnity of Our Lord Jesus Christ, Universal King, the fourth of the pontificate)

CHAPTER 14

'What did you go out in the wilderness to behold?' (Lk 7:24)

> When the messengers of John had gone, he [Jesus] began
> to speak to the crowds concerning John: "What did you go
> out into the wilderness to behold? A reed shaken by the
> wind? What then did you go out to see? A man clothed in
> soft raiment? Behold, those who are gorgeously appareled
> and live in luxury are in kings' courts. What then did you go
> out to see? A prophet? Yes, I tell you, and more than a
> prophet. This is he of whom it is written,
>> 'Behold, I send my messenger before thy face,
>> who shall prepare thy way before thee.'
> I tell you, among those born of women none is greater than
> John; yet he who is least in the kingdom of God is greater
> than he." (Luke 7:24-28)

SEVERAL YEARS ago I was completing my graduate studies
in philosophy at Tulane University. The director of my
thesis and my major professor is a man I admire enor-
mously. His seminars as well as our talks about my thesis
were very special. He was soon to retire from Tulane, and
I was privileged to be one of his last directees and members of his seminar. After my work was successfully completed, I worked up the courage to ask Professor Edward
G. Ballard the following question: "What do you consider
to be the most important lesson about life you have
learned to date? What piece of philosophical wisdom have
you gained from living and reflecting on your life?"

Professor Ballard leaned forward and straightened out his coat and tie. Whenever he did that, I knew something profound was about to come forth. It seemed like an hour, but it was only a few minutes until he finally said in his best Southern-gentlemanly drawl: "Father Maestri, over the years I've learned two important lessons that have lessened the pain of living and added to the joy of life."

At this point I expected him to quote Plato or Heidegger (the seminar for which he was most reputed). Instead of these or any of the other philosophical all-stars, I was given a vintage dose of Ballard. "After teaching for about ten years at this great university, I came to realize that I did not need to be the center of attention all of the time. I learned that my seminars, research and publications were not the only or the most important occurrences in the department or the university. At first this was not so. As a young teacher, I was going to write the great book and answer great questions. This is not bad for the young. It is necessary. But as St. Paul says. 'When I became a man, I gave up childish ways' (1 Cor 13:11). You become more realistic and appreciative of others. You come to see your life as part of a larger whole. The big dreams of youth can lead to big disappointments and resentment. If you're fortunate you make the transition to maturity and you come to experience a wider vision of life."

Professor Ballard leaned back in his chair as if he wanted to stand back from what he said (maybe in secret admiration!). He then leaned forward as if to whisper something very private and important. "Father Maestri, I also came to realize that if I do not have to be the focus of attention, and my work is not absolutely important — then I came to realize that I could let go of things in order to grow. It was painful, but I had to learn to explore new ideas and new areas of life if I was to make a contribution. You would think philosophers would be good at this. How-

ever, this is often not the case. We come to love our ideas
and views as if they are sacred and cannot be changed,
modified, or even replaced. We cling to them. We like to
say that they need us, but in reality it is we who need the
ideas, books, and students. The whole issue comes down to
ego and self-mastery. Not to be the center and to avoid
idol-making have been important principles for me in daily living. These did not come easy. And I must still be on
guard.''

I want to share the above story of Professor Ballard
because of what it means to me and the wisdom it contains. But I also want to share the episode because it beautifully captures the life of John the Baptizer. John is a
model who had to make room for another who would be
the center of history. John had to let go of his preaching,
baptisms, and disciples so that another could baptize with
fire and the Holy Spirit.

From the moment of John's existence he was destined
to play a significant role in salvation history. John's parents, Zechariah and Elizabeth, were childless. Elizabeth
was sterile, and now they were advanced in age. Yet it is
in situations of hopelessness and barrenness that God acts
on our behalf.

An angel appears to Zechariah and announces that
Elizabeth will bear a son who is to be called John. The
words of the angel offer a glimpse into the vocation of this
child strangely born: ''. . . for he will be great before the
Lord, and he shall drink no wine nor strong drink, and he
will be filled with the Holy Spirit, even from his mother's
womb. And he will turn many of the sons of Israel to the
Lord their God, and he will go before him in the spirit and
power of Elijah, to turn the hearts of fathers to the children and the disobedient to the wisdom of the just, to
make ready for the Lord a people prepared'' (Luke
1:14-17). Luke goes on to tell us that John had matured in

the ways of the Lord. John lived in the desert until the appointed time for him to appear in Israel and call the people to repentance.

The appearance of John was not quite what the people expected. St. Matthew tells us in his Gospel that "John wore a garment of camel's hair, and a leather girdle around his waist; and his food was locusts and wild honey" (Mt 3:4). If his dress and diet (he sounds like a product of the '60s, hooked on health foods!) were not enough to cause concern, his message was: "Repent, for the kingdom of heaven is at hand" (Mt 3:2). John even went so far as to trouble the comfortable and speak truth to power: "But when he saw many of the Pharisees and Sadducees coming for baptism, he said to them: 'You brood of vipers! Who warned you to flee from the wrath to come? Bear fruit that befits repentance, and do not presume to say to yourselves, "We have Abraham as our father." I tell you, God is able from these stones to raise up children to Abraham' " (Mt 3:7-9).

The Gospel writers go on to tell us that John was successful among the people. They came to him for baptism and the confession of their sins. John had a number of disciples who shared in his ministry. Yet we must be clear about this: the success and the actuation of those who became his disciples did not cloud his vision or move him to abandon his mission. John never lost sight of who he was and what role he was to play in the story of the Kingdom. Popularity and success did not blind him from seeing "the Lamb who takes away the sins of the world." John constantly reminded the people that he was not the Messiah. John always understood his vocation in light of the words of Isaiah:

> "The voice of one crying in the wilderness:
> Prepare the way of the Lord,
> make his paths straight.

Every valley shall be filled,
And every mountain and hill shall be brought low
and the crooked shall be made straight,
and the rough ways shall be made smooth;
and all flesh shall see the salvation of God" (Lk 2:4-6).

The Gospel of John provides a wonderful insight into the character of John. Jesus and John are in the same area, and their disciples are baptizing the people. The disciples of John come to him and complain that "all are going to him [Jesus]" (Jn 3:26). We might expect John to react with indignation. We might expect John to discredit Jesus and attack Him personally. However, John does none of this. John shows just how committed to God's work he is, and how unselfish his ministry. "No one can receive anything except what is given him from heaven" (Jn 3:27). If Jesus is winning over the people, it is part of God's plan. John, the good leader and pastor, is telling his followers that another is to assume the center stage. Another is to preach the mysteries of the Kingdom. The other one will baptize with the Holy Spirit and fire. John is not worthy to tie His shoes. John's consolation and joy are in doing God's will, seeing the Messiah, and leading others to the Lamb. Public recognition and popularity are not to stand in the way of the Messiah. John is the Messiah's herald. And he must not allow his own ego and the voices of others to stand in the way. John knows that he must grow less so Jesus can become more and more. Only love can do this!

The fidelity of John to his mission does not go unnoticed by Jesus. John prepared the way for the Messiah. Jesus now gives eloquent testimony concerning John. Jesus asks the crowds, "What did you go out in the wilderness to behold?" Some went out of curiosity. Some went to see a celebrity. Others went to trap John so he could be silenced. Jesus indicates that why some go looking for John

— hoping to influence him to be more moderate or sensible; to see someone with worldly influence and wealth; or to see a prophet who will see the future — are all the wrong reasons. There is only one reason that one goes to John — to have one's heart prepared for the coming Messiah. This means one must be willing to turn from sin and direct one's life toward the Kingdom. "What did you go out in the wilderness to behold?" There are as many answers as there are people to come to John. John is the faithful herald of the Messiah. The ultimate testimony concerning John comes from Jesus. Jesus says that John is a prophet and more. In the estimation of Jesus, "among those born of women none is greater than John."

Greatness in the service of the Gospel and fidelity to Jesus do not ensure the rewards of earthly greatness. Success in this world yields popularity, power, money, recognition, and all the benefits of the so-called "good life." Success ensures a guest spot on The Tonight Show or even Phil Donahue. However, fidelity to the Gospel and one's vocation yields a reward of a different kind. The reward is the Cross, and through it a share in eternal life. John has been faithful and selflessly loving. John never once got in the way of his message and his love, for God kept egoism in check. St. Mark tells the earthly end and the heavenly beginning of John. Herod ordered John arrested and silenced. John confronted Herod about living with Herodias, the wife of his brother Philip. Herodias wanted John killed for his words. At a banquet Herodias's daughter danced for Herod. He promised to give her anything, even half of his kingdom. At the urging of Herodias, she requested the head of John. Under the influence of a false sense of honor, Herod granted her request. John was beheaded. He dared to speak truth to power and paid the ultimate price. John lived for the glory of God rather than the praise of men. John knew that he would obey God rather than worldly principalities and powers. The death of John is really his rebirth and new beginning.

The place of John in salvation history is secure. The praise of Jesus for John's ministry is preserved in Scripture. Yet Jesus says that "he who is least the kingdom of heaven is greater than he." John would have understood and accepted this pronouncement by Jesus. The disciples of John must now follow Jesus. Why? Jesus is the ultimate word and revelation of God's love. The ultimate baptism is administered by Jesus and comes through His death and resurrection. Those who become disciples of Jesus and are reborn into the kingdom of God *are* greater than John. They are greater not because of the disciples' minds, but because of Jesus. And John's selfless love would accept and appreciate the insight.

The ministry of John the Baptizer has much to teach us about Christian discipleship. Let us reflect on just three aspects. Through baptism we are called to be *heralds* of Jesus Christ. In that part of the world we touch each day we are to bring Christ to others and see Christ in others. Baptism calls us to be messengers of God's unbounded love. We can feel so powerless and helpless in the face of sin and evil. Yet we can make a difference for the Kingdom. By our words and deeds we can be living and life-giving witnesses to the One who gives life in abundance. We can join together with fellow Christians to form a community of faith. We can bind up wounds, speak words of liberty, justice, and peace, visit the sick and imprisoned, and call the dead back to life. In the name of friendship and love we can work for change in our society so that all people are treated with dignity. We must respect life from the womb to the tomb. God continues to send messengers to prepare hearts for Him. Through baptism we are those messengers.

Baptism calls us to be witnesses for Christ. This can

never be taken lightly. The fate of John is the fate of every Christian. John's ministry reminds us of a second aspect of following Christ: we must be willing to face opposition and even death. The testimony of men and women who have paid the ultimate price fills the pages of Church history. Countless others have followed John in doing God's will rather than the will of men. In recent times we have the example of Dietrich Bonhoeffer, Maximilian Kolbe and the missionary women in El Salvador who gave their lives in service of the Gospel. Many others lay down their lives for others. Their sacrifices are not known to us. They are known to God alone. And He alone is the One who judges justly. Many lay down their lives daily in quiet and undramatic ways. They do for others without hope of reward or recognition. They place the needs of others above their own. Their only reward is in the knowledge that God's will is being done. These quiet heroes die to themselves each day and make room for others in their hearts. We daily encounter them in our homes, schools, offices, and as we walk down the street. And if you stopped them and recognized their work, they would be greatly surprised and a little embarrassed. For you see, they would probably indicate they were only doing their duty. Like John, they too do not need to be the center of life, and they know how to let go and move on.

The third aspect of John's ministry is the most important. All that he did and all that he was revolved around Jesus as the heart of his life and ministry. This is a crucial aspect for us today. Our baptism, preaching, teaching, and service are done out of love for Jesus Christ. The explicit love for Jesus, the service we do in His name, elevates our human love and service into the divine. Our thirsting after justice, seeking the road to peace, and respecting human rights are only possible when we acknowledge the sacredness of human life. Only when we acknowledge the common divine origin and destiny of human life can we have the realistic hope of defending all life. Only when we see Jesus in our brothers and sisters can we treat others as members of the one family of God. We are more than humanitarians and social activists. We are more than welfare workers and builders of a new secular world order. We belong to Christ and we want to lend our minds and hearts to building the New Jerusalem, a heavenly city not made by human hands. We want to help build the Kingdom of God. Without reference to God and Christ, our talk about human rights and justice remain like a noisy gong, a clanging cymbal. Only in a service to Jesus and the Kingdom do we have the realistic hope of making the world more just and peace-filled. Only in light of the Kingdom can we keep in check the idolatry of earthly powers from claiming ultimate authority. For the Christian there is only one in whose name we live and move and have our being — Jesus the Christ! In the words of the Apostle John: "As the branch cannot bear fruit by itself unless it abides in the vine, neither can you, unless you abide in me. . . . He who abides in me, and I in him, he it is that bears much fruit, for apart from me you can do nothing" (Jn 15:4-5).

"What did you go out in the wilderness to see?" This is not an idle question of Jesus. John was given a crucial role in salvation history, and his life is an eloquent testimony of fidelity to Jesus. Many went to see John out of curiosity; to see one strangely dressed; to silence him, or to see a great prophet. But for those who went to the river out of a spirit of repentance, whose hearts were prepared for the Messiah; for all who listened to John with an open heart, the rough spots were made smooth and the valleys filled in. The crooked roads were made straight and the various paths of life found their way to the One who is the Way and the Truth and the Life.

In the various situations of our life, we are to continue the ministry of John. We are to be heralds and messengers of the Lord who will return in glory. In the face of opposition or indifference, we proclaim the crucified and risen Lord. In times of inconvenience and the dark nights of the soul, we herald the One who comes in glory, the Light of Life. Each day is a down payment on eternity and a step closer to our true home. Let us pray for the courage to follow the example of John.

> O Lord help us to be your messengers and heralds in the world in which we live. Give us the wisdom to let Jesus be the center of our lives. Give us the power to love You above all things. Let our words and deeds be used by You to prepare the hearts of others. We are the least born in Your Kingdom. We come with our weaknesses and limitations. All that we have and hope to become is because of Your grace. As You inspired John and kept him faithful, do the same for us and Your Church. Let us not be as reeds swayed by the wind. We are not to be judged by the abundance of our possessions but by our fidelity to Jesus. Lead your Church not to the places of luxury and power but to Bethlehem, Golgotha, and the New Jerusalem. Amen.

CHAPTER 15

'Woman, where are they? Has no one condemned you?' (Jn 8:10)

> Early in the morning he came again to the temple; all the people came to him, and he sat down and taught them. The scribes and the Pharisees brought a woman who had been caught in adultery, and placing her in the midst they said to him, "Teacher, this woman has been caught in the act of adultery. Now in the law Moses commanded us to stone such. What do you say about her?" This they said to test him, that they might have some charge to bring against him. Jesus bent down and wrote with his finger on the ground. And as they continued to ask him, he stood up and said to them, "Let him who is without sin among you be the first to throw a stone at her." And once more he bent down and wrote with his finger on the ground. But when they heard it, they went away, one by one, beginning with the eldest, and Jesus was left alone with the woman standing before him. Jesus looked up and said to her, "Woman, where are they? Has no one condemned you?" She said, "No one, Lord." And Jesus said, "Neither do I condemn you; go, and do not sin again." (John 8:2-11)

ONE OF THE deepest longings and hopes of the human heart is the desire to start all over again. We have the need to believe and hope that rebirth, renewal, and redirection are possible in our lives. We need to know that the past is real but that it need not be the whole of reality. The past can be healed and transformed into a life-giving present and a hopeful future. Without the ability to hope and believe that yesterday need not determine today and tomorrow, we easily despair. We cash in our freedom and responsibility for the kind of persons we are made to be. The human being has the power to make today different from yesterday; and tomorrow need not be a carbon copy of our past or present. We can overcome the sins and failings of the past. We can experience a change of heart. We can be converted and healed through a covenant relationship with God's love and others.

Daily life is full of examples of those who refused to let their past be their whole identity and story: the young child who was born in the slums but refused to let the slums be born in him; the child from a poor rural setting who refused to let problems be excuses; the handicapped person who took problems and made them possibilities; the sinner who believed that God's love was greater than human failings — all of these and countless others give witness to new beginnings.

How are new beginnings possible? In the midst of my past, which seems so real and powerful, how can I start anew?

So many voices tell me I am bad, no good, and that I will never amount to anything. Significant others have labeled and libeled me as a sinner, a troublemaker, lazy, stupid, a dreamer, and countless other tags which have stuck to my consciousness. If so many see so little in me, how am I to see the good of even the hope of being more than I am at present? Let me offer an example of how destructive such voices can be in blinding one to present possibilities and future happiness.

Jane is an attractive, well-educated, and seemingly happily married young woman with a good husband and a two-year-old daughter. Jim is an engineer and makes a very comfortable living for Jane and their daughter Kathy. Up until the time of Kathy's arrival, Jane was an

English teacher in a Catholic high school. One day Jane came to see me and told the following story.

"Father Maestri, I do not know quite how to say this, but I've been unfaithful to Jim. I've been seeing another man."

Jane was in perfect control. She seemed determined not to cry or even appear upset. It was as if she were speaking about another person. I asked how long she had been seeing this other man, and she said, "About six months or so."

I was somewhat surprised by her lack of definiteness and seeming indifference. Before I could ask another question she said, "And you know, I really don't love him. I don't even know why I am doing this to Jim and Kathy."

I couldn't help but ask, "Are you doing this to Jim and Kathy?"

That response struck her as strange. "Of course I am hurting Jim and Kathy. Who else is involved?"

If my question struck her as strange, then her response left me very amazed. "What about you? Aren't you being hurt by this relationship?"

She looked somewhat surprised and said, "Me? Yes, I guess I am being hurt. But that is to be expected."

"Why is it expected that *you* are to be hurt? Where is it written that others should be protected but Jane is fair game?"

A long time passed before she answered me. She kept looking at her wedding ring and turning it around her finger. Finally she offered the following:

"So many people would envy me. I have a loving husband. I have a beautiful child. I have so much to be thankful for."

"Then, Jane," I said, "why can't you be happy? Do you feel you don't deserve happiness?"

Jane raised her head and said in a voice filled with anger and hurt, "Of course I deserve to be happy! But I'll never be happy. My parents told me long ago I would hurt others like I hurt them. They told me I would disappoint everyone and everything I touched. I am doing a good job, don't you think?"

It was now my turn to be silent. Jane sat there doing her best to fight back tears of anger and hurt. I finally asked, "Why did your parents say such things?"

In a soft, almost inaudible voice, Jane responded: "I've never pleased my parents. Nothing I did or do is right. I went to the wrong schools. I wasn't queen of the prom. And according to them, I didn't marry the right man. I don't know if there ever was a Mr. Right. But according to them, Jim isn't the one."

Jane went on to recount that her sister was much more acceptable to her parents. Beth was still living at home and pretty much doing the bidding of her parents. Beth was now dating. She had a good job in a college bookstore. Jane did not resent Beth. She did not seem to have any real feelings about Beth.

The story of Jane is not uncommon. The voices of significant others and the power of the past are strong. Too many people are imprisoned by the negative and destructive expectations of others. We feel we must live out the script that others write for us. Jane's parents had long ago told her she would amount to nothing, be destructive, and hurt the ones she loves. No one is excusing Jane and her infidelity. She bears responsibility for her actions. However, we need to understand that our zone of freedom and subsequent responsibility is not a zero-sum game. There are many factors at work to enhance and restrict our freedom. The early voices of parents, teachers, and all who comprise our significant others make a real difference. These early voices can help in our growth toward maturity; or these voices can be a stumbling block.

I will end the story of Jane by simply saying that she has broken off her extramarital relationship. She has been receiving excellent spiritual and psychological direction. She still has attacks of self-doubt and destruction, but Jane is making progress. And in the game of life, a little progress is a lot of progress.

The story of Jane indicates how important and influential we are for one another. Our words and deeds make a real difference in the present and for the future. The words we say to one another and the stories we write with those words must be done with love and care. Naturally, not everyone must deal with a story and parents like Jane. Also, even when one inherits a destructive story from significant others, redemption is possible. It is possible to begin anew and start all over. Our past can be accepted and reconciled. Forgiveness, healing, and new life are always possible. If, and that is a very big *if*, we are to turn our lives around and experience redemption, we must be fortunate enough to meet a *redeeming other*. We must encounter a person or community who accepts our past and gives us hope for the future. We need to be wise and courageous enough to let go of our past and march into the future. At times we can become comfortable with our demons and even make peace with them. At times we resist change and a new beginning at all costs. But if, again that word *if*, we want to change and begin anew, such is possible.

The story of the woman caught in adultery is a powerful example of letting go of the past, accepting forgiveness in the present, and going forward with confidence for the future. Biblical scholars tell us that this story was not part of the original Johannine manuscript and was added at a later date. These scholars go on to speculate that the story probably belongs to the Gospel of St. Luke. Regardless of these important questions, we can say that this story is part of Scripture and certainly worthy of our prayerful consideration.

The Pharisees and scribes bring a woman caught in adultery to Jesus as a test case of His orthodoxy. The Law is simple and straightforward: the woman caught in adultery must be stoned. To say otherwise would be to place oneself against the teachings of Moses. Unlike the questions of Jesus, the questions of the Pharisees are destructive, anti-life, and posed only in order to trap and condemn. The goal of the Pharisees' questions is not truth but their own power and privilege. Jesus at first refuses to play their game and ignores their question. However, the Pharisees continue to question Jesus about His views concerning this adulterous woman. The legalistic and self-righteous mind-set does not give up easily. The Pharisees' question of entrapment is answered by Jesus with a response of genius: "Let him who is without sin among you be the first to throw a stone at her." They all walk away. Only God is without sin. All of us have fallen short of the glory of God. What is most upsetting to the Pharisees is not the adulterous woman getting off but the fact that they were unable to trap Jesus.

We are now drawn into one of the most moving encounters between Jesus and another person. The woman is left alone in the presence of Jesus. We can only speculate as to her thoughts. What would He say? What would He do? What is this Rabbi up to? Maybe the stones of the Pharisees would have been easier to take! No doubt this woman's past came rushing painfully into the present. The feelings of guilt and shame caused as much pain as any stone hitting the flesh. How much did Jesus know? What could she say to soften His response? Maybe she could excuse herself out of the situation?

At this point Jesus asks where her accusers and judges are. They have all gone away. The woman stands in the presence of the One who accuses and condemns no one. She is in the presence of the Judge who judges justly by weighing the quality of one's heart. Jesus has not come to condemn but to give life in abundance. Jesus comes as the Father's love letter to all people that the long reign of sin will not ultimately win out. Life is stronger than death. The past need not imprison us and keep us from living life to the full. In Jesus it is possible to start again and live anew. Guilt, shame, and sin need not have the final word in our lives. Jesus is about reconciliation, not condemnation; new beginnings, and not past failings.

Does all of this talk about reconciliation, redemption, and new beginnings mean that sin is not to be taken seriously? Is Jesus being soft on sin? Wouldn't it be proper for Jesus to have "laid down the moral law" to this adulterous woman? The answer to these questions is *no*. The atonement won by Jesus comes at the price of His suffering love revealed on the cross. Jesus defeats the destructive power of sin by the life-giving power of love. Jesus is anything but soft on sin. In fact, it would be much easier to read this woman the Mosaic Law and fill her with guilt. But then what? What would the future hold in light of the past? To simply lay down the law is to misuse the law as a weapon. There is no real hope of redemption.

Jesus does not condemn, but He challenges in this way to accept her acceptance. Jesus is challenging this woman to let go of the past and move on into the future. What is done is done. The past is real. Adultery is real. However, one need not be an adulteress forever. Jesus tells the woman she may "go." Go where? This woman is being given the opportunity to leave the past, the guilt, and all of the angry words and accusations of the past few moments. The accusers and judges have vanished. The past needs to be healed as well. Jesus is offering this woman another chance to walk into tomorrow.

Jesus overcomes the power of the past through the power of nonjudgmental, accepting love. The Pharisees and scribes see in this woman only an adulteress and a chance to trap Jesus. This woman is not a peson in need of healing or worthy of respect. She is a sinner and deserves a good stoning. By contrast, Jesus accepts *totally* the person in need of healing. Jesus does not excuse her past. He does not trivialize her behavior or minimize her real guilt and shame. If she is to experience redemption she must also accept responsibility for her past. Only in this atmosphere of nonjudgmental, accepting love can this woman be challenged to avoid this sin from now on. Only in an atmosphere in which our dignity is respected can we respect ourselves enough to turn things around. It is only *after* Jesus accepts this woman as a person that she can accept the challenge to live in a new way. If we do not experience initial acceptance and respect, we can never move on with life. We continue to be hounded by the past and labor under the burdens of guilt.

The reconciling and redemptive work of Jesus continues with the Church. The sacrament of reconciliation is our explicit encounter with redemption and the forgiving love of Jesus Christ. Through the sacrament of reconciliation we are invited to acknowledge our sinfulness and weakness. We can risk such disclosures because God is love and the love of God comes to us through this sacrament. Not only can we risk acknowledging our past failures, but we can live in a new way. The sacrament of reconciliation draws us into God's forgiving love and empowers us to live no longer for ourselves alone but for God and neighbors. The grace received in this sacrament does more than wipe the slate clean or wash away the dark spots. The grace of reconciliation opens for us the real possibility of a *metanoia* or conversion. The sacrament of reconciliation affords us the opportunity to direct our whole lives to the love of God. The grace of reconcilation opens our hearts to God as the origin, ground, and goal of our existence. There is always the danger of sin in our lives. There is always the danger of turning our hearts away from God in favor of some earthly creature or goal. Hence, not only is reconciliation the forgiveness of past sins but a strengthening for the future.

Whenever the sacrament of reconciliation is discussed, questions arise: "Why do I have to go to a priest and confess my sins?" "Why can't I go directly to God?" "The priest is a human being just like me, so why should I tell another human what I have done?" It is easy to dismiss these questions. However, they deserve a response. God's revelation of Himself is for the most part a mediated or secondary revelation. That is, God makes Himself known through the natural world or created order. The events of history — for example, the Exodus experience in the Old Testament — tell us something about God. God uses and works through the finite to reveal the infinite. Salvation is mediated through the Word who becomes flesh. Salvation is achieved through the death and resurrection of Jesus. Jesus is the ultimate mediator between God and humankind. Jesus is the "go-between" in the story of reconciliation. The mystery of God's love becomes visible in the person of Jesus.

The mediation of salvation and the encounter of God's forgiving love continue through the sacrament of reconciliation. The priest is the instrument of mediation between God and the individual seeking forgiveness. God comes to us through the humanity of Jesus, and we return to God through the humanity of the priest and our own humanity. We vocalize our sins and lay claim to our personal responsibility. The priest accepts these sins as part of our life in need of healing. In accepting our sins, the priest also pronounces the words of forgiveness and hope. The priest, human and in need of forgiveness as well, pronounces the words of liberation and peace. There is a human need to hear the words of forgiveness, release, and hope. "Your sins are forgiven. Go in peace" — these are words that have power. These words continue the story of the Word who became flesh.

Finally, the ministry of reconciliation is not limited to the priest and the confessional. St. Paul, writing to the Christians at Corinth, beautifully expresses the ministry of reconciliation to which we are all called.

> Therefore if any one is in Christ, he is a new creation; the old has passed away, behold, the new has come. All this is from God, who through Christ reconciled us to himself and gave us the ministry of reconciliation; that is, God was in Christ reconciling the world to himself, not counting their trespasses against them, and entrusting to us the message of reconciliation. So we are ambassadors for Christ, God making his appeal through us. We beseech you on behalf of Christ, he reconciled to God. For our sake he made him to be sin who knew no sin, so that in him he might become the righteousness of God. (2 Cor 5:17-21)

All of us through baptism are ambassadors for Christ. We are the living agents of God's reconciling work. In those parts of the world we touch each day, we can bring the reconciling love of God. So many today are in need of forgiveness and reconciliation. Many groups and individuals in the Church are in need of healing. Divorced and separated Catholics, those who have had abortions, conservatives and liberals, young and old, clergy and lay, black, white, Asian, Hispanic — all these are in need of reconciliation. Many of our Catholic brothers and sisters are in need of the kiss of peace, the oil of gladness, and the embrace of acceptance. This doesn't mean we accept everything another says or does. It does not mean that we don't face many doctrinal and pastoral problems. But none of these differences and problems are greater than that which unites us — the love of Jesus.

The ministry of reconciliation means we must take risks and creatively respond to the Holy Spirit. The woman caught in adultery and Jesus' response are crucial for us today. That woman encountered what she most needed, not a voice of condemnation but one of forgiveness and challenge. Jesus was not deterred by the voices of self-righteousness and moralistic indignation. Jesus risked a creative response. He believed that this woman was more than her past and that she could be more in the future. What she needed was someone to believe in her, accept her, love her, and challenge her. She found all this in Jesus. And her life would never be the same. That is the miracle of reconciliation. That is the miracle each of us can receive and each of us can give.

EPILOGUE

'Can the wedding guests fast while the bridegroom is with them?' (Mk 2:19)

Now John's disciples and the Pharisees were fasting; and people came and said to [Jesus], "Why do John's disciples and the disciples of the Pharisees fast, but your disciples do not fast?" And Jesus said to them, "Can the wedding guests fast while the bridegroom is with them? As long as they have the bridegroom with them, they cannot fast. The days will come, when the bridegroom is taken away from them, and then they will fast in that day. No one sews a piece of unshrunk cloth on an old garment; if he does, the patch tears away from it, the new from the old, and a worse tear is made. And no one puts new wine into old wineskins; if he does, the wine will burst the skins, and the wine is lost, and so are the skins; but new wine is for fresh skins. (Mark 2:18-22)

WE HAVE COME a long way in our discussion concerning the questions of Jesus. These questions have been directed to different individuals and groups: fishermen, disciples, sinners, the self-righteous, those burdened by guilt, those in need of healing, and each of us. The questions of Jesus are not frozen in space and time. There is a timeless and timely quality about them. These questions invite us to reflect on the meaning of our lives, the destiny of our existence, the mission of the Church and the cost of discipleship. We have reflected on some of the most important needs of the human condition and the ways in which God cares for

157

those needs: forgiveness, healing, atonement, and resurrection. We live in a world vastly different from first-century Palestine. However, the questions of Jesus challenge the human heart across the centuries to accept God's unbounded love and to share that love each day. The questions of Jesus continue to have "cash value" for those who watch TV, fly in an airplane, and venture into outer space.

Our final question in many ways serves to sum up all that has gone before. Jesus asks, "How can the guests at a wedding fast as long as the groom is still among them?" In effect, Jesus is asking us if we can be individuals and a community of joy, celebration, and hope. The way in which we respond to this question sums up the ways we have responded to Jesus' questions in past chapters. The question of joy is a "single-issue" test by which to judge our relationship with Jesus.

Admittedly, the topic of joy is not an easy one to advance. The doom-and-gloom boom is all around us. Unfortunately, too much of the boom is going on in so-called Christian communities. Angry video vicars, preachers of destruction, and the Christian in the pew who is turned off to life — all these stand in contradiction to the joy Jesus came to give us. We can only wonder how many find the Christian story unbelievable because we Christians find joy unbelievable. The story of the German philosopher and atheist Friedrich Wilhelm Nietzsche (1844-1900) offers a powerful example.

Nietzche's father was a Lutheran pastor, and Friedrich was required to attend services and hear his father preach. One day after services Nietzsche was reported to have said to his sister, "Why don't Christians look more redeemed?" Maybe if Nietzsche had experienced more joy and known Christians who acted more redeemed, his life would have been less tragic and painful. Maybe Nietzsche would have come to a conclusion other than his oft-quoted dictum, "God is dead!" I often wonder how many Christians leave their places of worship and ask what Nietzsche asked, "Why don't Christians look more redeemed?" Our worship can be a model of liturgical correctness, beautiful music, good reading (no small achievement), and even good sermons (now maybe I am asking too much), but if our worship lacks joy and celebration it is a noisy gong and clanging cymbal. Only a worship that is led by a joyful celebrant, and one in which the community joyfully participates, is fitting for Yahweh-Jesus.

Dismal faces and gloomy saints are not peculiar to the modern world or the post-Vatican II Church. Like the poor, the joyless have always been with us. Jesus in the Sermon on the Mount reminds the crowd they are "not to look glum" (Mt 6:16). In our Gospel reading that opened this Epilogue, we see Jesus having to contend with those who feel that He is not somber enough about religion. They feel that a little more fasting and sacrifice are in order. They appeal to the Golden Age of John the Baptizer, who required his disciples to fast. Jesus seems to be advocating a dangerous liberalization which will destroy discipline. Jesus doesn't seem to be taking sin seriously, and what is needed to overcome evil.

There have always been voices in the Christian community advocating a circling of the wagons, drawing lines in the dirt, and getting tough with sin. Joy and celebration seem out of place and downright dangerous. There has always been a kind of nostalgia for a Golden Age when sin was in retreat and God walked with humankind in the cool of the day. Naturally, there is a danger that joy and celebration can degenerate into frenzy and orgy. St. Paul had to contend with joy becoming corrupt and used as an excuse for carnal excess (see 1 Cor 11:17ff; Eph 5:18, etc.). However, the misuse of joy is no argument against its proper place in the Christian life. The Christian is essentially a person of joy, hope, and celebration. The Christian does not look backward for some Paradise Lost or Eden to regain, but we look to the future and the full coming of God's Kingdom.

In the name of hard-headed realism, isn't this talk about joy and celebration a symptom of being tender-hearted (what is really meant is that one is "soft-headed")? To speak about joy and celebration in the closing decades of the twentieth century seems to deny the every-day realities of television and newspaper: war and the rumors of war; murders or attempted assassinations of diplomats and pop stars, priests and nuns, bishops, popes, and presidents; hatred in the Middle East, Northern Ireland, and Latin America; urban violence, energy and ecology crises, the divorce rate, domestic violence — and the list goes on, suggesting anything but joy and celebration. If anything, we should take a cue from Jonah and John the Baptizer: don sackcloth and ashes, fast, do penance, and repent.

While it would be foolish to deny the demonic in history and the darkness in the human heart, the above is by no means the total picture. We must be willing to broaden our vision to include the greatness and nobility of the human spirit. The human story is not one of just weeds, evil deeds, and the love of darkness. History also tells a story of heroism, unselfish love, and the willingness to transcend egoism and pride. The nearness of our everyday lives contains rumors of angels and signals of transcendence (Peter Berger) that speak of humanity's finer moments. The lives of the saints speak to us of men and women in whom God's love became visible. We all know men and women who each day reach out to others in love, forgiveness, acceptance, and place the needs of others before their own. We all know people who labor daily to build a better world without hope of recognition and reward.

We are aware of the enormous problems that face us today. However, we must also be aware of the ascent of the human family. The advances in medicine, political freedom, economic growth, social equality, and a renewed sense of reverence for the environment give cause for hope. Naturally, we have much to do, but this should not blind us to the much that has been done. History is filled with the ugliness of the human condition. Yet so much of our everyday life is wrapped in beauty: the smile of a friend, the touch of a child, the breeze on a summer day after a rainstorm, the vastness of space. These and all the "dappled things" (G.M. Hopkins) speak to us of the mystery of existence and God's love.

Where does all this leave us? What are we to make of human history and the human condition? Human existence is a mystery that combines the capacity for great nobility and awful evil. This means we must take a stance, a wager if you will, a risk, concerning the way we live each day. Like Shakespeare's Macbeth, we can look at history and our everyday world as "a tale / told by an idiot, full of sound and fury, / signifying nothing," or we can approach life as a gift, a mysterious gift but a gift nonetheless. Life can be viewed as having a meaning and goal that transcend the passing moment. The tragedy and evil of history can be viewed as real but not ultimately real. God's love is at work, transforming and healing the present on the way to the Kingdom. God's love has the last, best word.

The American philosopher William James told us we have a "right to believe." We also have a right not to believe. But let us be clear about our decision. The way we place our bets concerning the meaning of life has real consequences in the way we live each day. If life is short, cruel, and absurd, then so is my individual life. Hence I am more likely to live for the moment and grab for the gusto: life is a short-term contest in which I compete with others and get what I can out of this absurd world; death is the final statement about life, and so there is no right and wrong, just whatever gets me through to the next day; suicide is always an option if the pain of living becomes too burdensome.

On the other hand, if I accept life as a gift and try to find the beauty that does surround me, then I live each day in gratitude. I do not merely seek pleasure and avoid pain, but I share my gifts with others. I see the other person not as an adversary or a competitor but as a neighbor and friend. The other person is not a threat but a gift. While death is real, it is not the Really Real. While much of life is cruel and absurd, the whole story in the long view says something different: life is worth living, and my individual existence counts and makes a difference; instead of suicide, I choose life and hope.

How does the Christian come down on the question of life? Do we live today and face tomorrow as celebrators, with hope and joy? Or do we merely survive from day to day, just waiting for the end because that is all there is? Ever since that first Easter Sunday when the angel said that the Living One is not to be found among the dead, the answer is obvious: we cannot help but celebrate and live each day with hope and joy. The Crucified One is now risen. The tomb that held Jesus is now empty. In the words of St. Paul:

> This perishable nature must put on the imperishable, and this mortal nature must put on immortality. When the perishable put on the imperishable, and the mortal puts on immortality, then shall come to pass the saying that is written: "Death is swallowed up in victory."
> "O death, where is thy victory?
> O death, where is thy sting?"
> The sting of death is sin, and the power of sin is the law. But thanks be to God, who gives us the victory, through our Lord Jesus Christ. (1 Cor 15:53-57)

Jesus has won for us the ultimate victory. Death is not stronger than life. Despair does not have the last word, but hope. And the absurdity of life gives way to the ultimate meaning of God's life-giving love.

The question of Jesus contains the answer for how we are to face life. If Golgotha was the final episode about Jesus, then we should persist in our fasting, in gloom, doom, and disillusionment; death and sin continue to have the upper hand, and we must wait for another. But Jesus is the Messiah who comes to bring life in abundance. Jesus is the bridegroom who comes to call the guests to the wedding banquet of the Kingdom. Hence we cannot help but celebrate and be joyful. Jesus tells the crowd there is an appropriate time for fasting. However, the Messiah has come and the Kingdom has broken into history. What the prophets and Abraham longed to see has now made its appearance. The Word has become flesh, and the love of God has been made visible. How can one not celebrate!

A new question arises: But hasn't Jesus been taken from us? Jesus has ascended to the Father, and we are awaiting His return in glory. That is not a new question, but one that has troubled the Church from the beginning. The answer from Scripture is important. Jesus *continues* to be with His people through the indwelling of the Paraclete. Jesus has not left us orphans but remains with us through the Holy Spirit. The Spirit abides in the heart of the disciple and the community of disciples proclaiming Jesus as Lord. In John 14, the disciples are filled with sadness at the approaching death of Jesus. But He reassures them, ". . . you will be sorrowful, but your sorrow will turn into joy" (Jn 16:20). The disciples will know the joy of the risen Lord. St. Luke, opening the Acts of the Apostles, tells us that the disciples must move beyond fear and passivity.

Granted, the physical presence of Jesus is gone.

However, the Spirit is sent at Pentecost. The disciples are to be the witnesses of Jesus to the whole world.

The reflections above about joy and celebration can lead one to the erroneous conclusion that the concerns of social justice are unimportant. Quite the contrary. It is precisely because Yahweh and Jesus call us to celebrate and be joyful that the cries of the poor, the oppressed, and the marginals are so pressing a problem. The wretched of the earth are so important because they too are precious in God's eyes and are our brothers and sisters. Our celebrations and liturgies are always incomplete as long as Lazarus sits ignored outside our gate. Our celebrations and joy are moderated each time the dignity of one human being is ignored. All men and women are called to celebrate the experience of God's unbounded love. The Spirit dwells in the heart of the poor. In fact, Jesus tells us that the poor, the sick, the lonely, and the imprisoned are special opportunities to meet Him. The Yahweh-Jesus stories of God call us to celebrate and experience joy. At the same time, these stories of God (John Shea) challenge us to eliminate all those things that keep our neighbor from the joyful celebration of the gift of life.

Jesus the Bridegroom is within us through the Holy Spirit. We cannot help but celebrate and be joyful. We cannot help but go forth and tell the world what God has done for us. The gift of earthly life is but a foretaste and promise of that heavenly wedding banquet of eternal life. In the Gospel of John is recorded the last will and testament of Jesus just before He dies. We might imagine a statement of anger about the unfairness of life and how friends prove to be enemies. We might imagine words of self-righteous indignation about the corrupt civil and religious authorities. We might also expect Jesus to be sad and depressed. Yet St. John records in these chapters (14-17) a picture of Jesus that is quite different from our expectations. Jesus accepts the disciples' fear and sense of gloom. He knows they are weak and need strengthening. Jesus challenges the disciples to move beyond this hour of darkness. He challenges the disciples to be courageous enough to celebrate and be joyful.

> When a woman is in travail [labor] she has sorrow, because her hour has come; but when she is delivered of the child she no longer remembers the anguish, for joy that a child is born into the world. So you have sorrow now, but I will see you again and your hearts will rejoice, and no one will take your joy from you. (Jn 16:21-22)

The Christian story proclaims that death gives way to life; despair to hope; and sadness to joy. The question of Jesus is for us: "Can the wedding guests fast while the groom is with them?" Jesus is with us and within us. Jesus will come again in glory. How do I answer Jesus? How do we? How do *you*?